"It is clear that Ryan Romeo is passion[...] Jesus and to see the church at the foref[...] With his new book, Ryan looks to motivate local churches across the world toward unity and to rise up, have faith, and reach their communities."

Chad Veach

Author of Unreasonable Hope

"Ryan Romeo's heart beats for the LOCAL church. His passion goes so far beyond a platform, an event, or one solitary ministry. He has a passion to see the unification of God's people globally to support what happens locally."

Mack Brock

Elevation Worship

"Ryan Romeo shows us love for the church—God's love for the church. Romeo reminds us that Jesus gave his life for the church. So we, too, are called to love the bride of Christ (since we, too, are the bride of Christ, and self-hate is not healthy). May God rekindle our love for *his* love. And may God renew the church for *his* glory."

Tom Parker

Fuller Theological Seminary

"Ryan Romeo's love and commitment to the local church should inspire us all. Truly the greatest impact we can have in our city is when we put our selfish ambitions aside and say yes to being part of the body of Christ. Ryan is living proof of that."

Cody Williams

Director of Development at Jesus Culture

"Ryan and company make a beautiful case for this generation to be romanced by the movement of assembled Christ followers called the local church. *OUTCRY* declares God's power and our mission and responsibility as the church under that authority. Find your heart, no matter the condition, wooed into this movement. No wonder his last name is Romeo."

Eric Samuel Timm

Orator, Artist, Author, Visionary

"God's plan has always been the local church. Ryan Romeo beautifully illuminates that narrative and deciphers the meaning of who we are and what God is doing through us as his body. I'm so encouraged by this book about the beauty of the local church. Be ready to be challenged and encouraged."

Jeff Gokee

Executive Director of PHOENIX/ONE

"*OUTCRY* illuminates the amazing movement of Jesus within the church across the globe! The Holy Spirit has beautifully spoken through Ryan Romeo to give us hope and assurance that the power of God is on the move!"

Gebben Miles

Multiple World Champion Clay Target Shooter and Coach

OUTCRY

NEW VOICES SPEAK OUT ABOUT
THE POWER OF THE CHURCH

RYAN ROMEO

WORTHY®
PUBLISHING

Published by Worthy Books, an imprint of Worthy Publishing Group, a division of Worthy Media, Inc., One Franklin Park, 6100 Tower Circle, Suite 210, Franklin, TN 37067.

WORTHY is a registered trademark of Worthy Media, Inc.

HELPING PEOPLE EXPERIENCE THE HEART OF GOD

eBook available wherever digital books are sold.

Library of Congress Cataloging-in-Publication Data

Names: Romeo, Ryan, author.
Title: Outcry : new voices speak out about the power of the church / Ryan
    Romeo.
Description: Franklin, TN : Worthy Pub., 2016.
Identifiers: LCCN 2016018056 | ISBN 9781617957536 (tradepaper)
Subjects: LCSH: Mission of the church. | Christianity and culture.
Classification: LCC BV601.8 .R65 2016 | DDC 250--dc23
LC record available at https://lccn.loc.gov/2016018056

For foreign and subsidiary rights, contact rights@worthypublishing.com

ISBN: 978-1-61795-753-6 (paperback)

Printed in the United States of America
16 17 18 19 20 BVG 8 7 6 5 4 3 2 1

OUTCRY

WITH CONTRIBUTIONS FROM

SHANE QUICK ✦ *OUTCRY*

DAVID CROWDER

JENN JOHNSON ✦ *Bethel Music*

CHRIS QUILALA ✦ *Jesus Culture*

PAT BARRETT ✦ *Housefires*

CHRIS LLEWELLYN ✦ *Rend Collective*

To my wife, Blake, for her tireless support.
I would never have been able to write this without her.

✦

To my dad, who taught me to never give up on a dream.

✦

To my mom, who always believed I could do more.

✦

To Shane Quick for our countless hours
of audacious dreaming.

✦

And to my church, Living Streams, for their inspiration,
prayer, and support of me and my family.

CONTENTS

FOREWORD

KARI JOBE AND CODY CARNES

One night during the Spring 2016 OUTCRY Tour, I had a dream. In this dream, I was walking around a beautiful, ornate old church with gorgeous architecture. And inside were these long wooden pews filled with people. Inside the building it was actually raining, and the people sitting didn't seem to notice. As I walked around, I noticed that there were about four inches of water splashing up on my shoes. It was very clean and beautiful water that seemed to be flowing by itself in different directions. The water felt cleansing. It felt light and peaceful. There was no heaviness in the room. The water seemed to be cleaning and renewing everything in the church.

I feel like this is God's dream for us as a church in this season. In Ephesians 5:26–27, Paul talks about Jesus returning for a spotless bride (the church), who has been cleansed with water. Cleansed with the Word. I believe this is what God is doing.

OUTCRY has a simple message: It's about the local church. It's about the one movement called the church. And OUTCRY is just a megaphone for what God is already doing in each city it enters. Even the logo, the kid standing at the megaphone, is a depiction of the church. God's already been doing amazing things through the church. It's happening all around us. But these OUTCRY tour nights are inspiring and refreshing. Encouraging the pastors and church leaders to keep going—to let them know that they are making a difference.

In many ways, I believe we are experiencing the fruit of the prayers of our parents—the prayers of the previous generation for our generation. There were seeds sown into me as a young girl that are bearing fruit now. And I want to honor how they led me and how they will lead the next generation into a new chapter in the church.

—Kari Jobe Carnes

About halfway through the spring 2016 OUTCRY tour, I opened my Bible app to the verse of the day. And it happened to be the passage Romans 15:5–7, which talks about unity—that when we accept one another and love each other the way that Jesus loves us, God is glorified. When I read that, it really hit me: This is why we are doing what we do with OUTCRY. We want to remind people that we are stronger and better *together*.

I believe there is a lie that has infiltrated the church for too long: that our differences are more important than our unity under the name of Jesus and that those differences have to keep us apart. So if God is glorified by unity, then of course the enemy's strategy would be division. It is hard to accept people who are different from us. But Jesus extended grace to us when we didn't deserve it. He extended acceptance and family to us even when we were still in sin. And Jesus gives us that same power of love and acceptance of one another in the body, if we allow him. People consistently ask, "How can I glorify God more in my life?" Unity, a genuine love for one another, is one of the ways we can.

In John 17, Jesus says that the world will know him by the love we have for one another. Think about that. If everyone in the body of Christ were loving and accepting of one another, who wouldn't want to be a part of a family like that? I think the church is entering a season of understanding the power of unity more and more.

Unity doesn't mean that we are all the same. Jesus calls the church his *body*. Now, in my body, my foot and my hand have to function in different ways, but they both agree that they're a part of the same body—with the understanding that working in agreement is best. In the body of Christ, that agreement is under the banner of Jesus. The church has many different parts playing different roles, and that's beautiful. It's through those differences that we can experience diverse aspects of God's character. And that's why we can celebrate our differences.

I remember during one of our nights at OUTCRY, I went out in the crowd. I found myself imagining that this was my city, my community, and that the people around me represented churches in my town. And I found myself welling up with encouragement. I began thinking, *These are my brothers and sisters. These are the people God has given me to walk with and change this city.* The enemy wants to tell us that we are alone. He wants us feeling disconnected and isolated. But nights like OUTCRY help everyone see that we aren't on our own. We are all in this together. And that is a powerful thing.

I hope people understand that OUTCRY is more than a concert. It's not just a cool night to hear creative music. It's so much more than that! It's a celebration of Jesus and his church. Your horizons widen when you see many believers in your city come together—no matter the denomination. God wants to make a deposit in each of these cities. He has something special in each of these communities. Each night, he brings us all to a new level together. We can't wait to see what he does with the new seeds that are being planted in these cities every night.

—Cody Carnes

IN A SINGLE MOMENT

In a single moment everything changed. Out of the void of nothingness came everything. Suddenly there was light, matter, space, and time. In that explosive moment the universe came into being. The laws of physics and mathematics were created. Gravitational pull began to collect matter into celestial bodies. Stars, galaxies, solar systems, and planets.

Chemistry came into being. Water and air. Oceans and land.

The moon and sun hung in the sky. Morning and evening. Night and day.

Life exploded. Plants and animals. Man and woman.

And at the center of it all was him. He was there and caused it to be. By his voice it all came into being. From the very beginning, before time and space, he was there. And he was the catalyst, that by his very word the explosion of creation was set into motion.

In the beginning was the Word, and the Word was with God, and the Word was God. He was with God in the beginning. Through him all things were made; without him nothing was made that has been made. In him was life, and that life was the light of all mankind. The light shines in the darkness, and the darkness has not overcome it. (John 1:1–5)

Jesus. The light of mankind. The creator of everything out of nothing.

The words of Jesus are powerful things. By the very words that he spoke, creation came into being. Everything we can see, hear, and touch began with him. Not only that, but the intangible was created: joy, creativity, and covenant. Our ability to *see* creation and find beauty in it. All set off by Jesus's word.

But this isn't the last time he set such a cataclysmic event into motion with the sound of his voice. There was another moment on earth that was just as explosive. Just as significant. And though it seems less dramatic, could it be that it is even *more* consequential?

"You are Peter, a rock. *This is the rock on which I will put together my church, a church so expansive with energy that not even the gates of hell will be able to keep it out.* And that's not all. You will have complete and free access to God's kingdom, keys to open any and every door: no more barriers between heaven and earth, earth and heaven. A yes on earth is yes in heaven. A no on earth is no in heaven." (Matthew 16:17–19 MSG, emphasis added)

I will build my church. The church. His movement. Our movement.

With the sound of his voice he set it into motion. He began a movement with all of the same diversity and creativity he used in creation. Not only that, but he gave this movement unprecedented power. Not simply to Peter. Peter was just the beginning of a movement filled with expansive power. His power. Jesus gave *us* the keys to heaven. He gave us complete access to his kingdom. To him. He said that the gates of hell cannot keep back our onslaught. The *defense* of the enemy won't withstand our *offense*. It cannot prevail.

Later Jesus spoke again. His final words here on Earth were to his disciples, commissioning them. Sending them out with vision and purpose. Passing on the singular mission that would catalyze the greatest revolution in history. And he commissioned us with the same vision.

> Then Jesus came to them and said, "All authority in heaven and on earth has been given to me. Therefore go and make disciples of all nations, baptizing them in the name of the Father and of the Son and of the Holy Spirit, and teaching them to obey everything I have commanded you. And surely I am with you always, to the very end of the age." (Matthew 28:18–20)

In a single moment he commissioned his disciples to start his movement. He didn't write a book. He didn't hold in-depth how-to-do-church seminars. He didn't even stay with them until the day of Pentecost. He simply lived his life with the disciples and left them with the immense task of *starting*.

Ten days later the Holy Spirit showed up in power and caused amazing growth and expansion of the kingdom.

Three thousand people were saved the first time the disciples preached about Jesus. This is an incredible way to start the story.

The story of the church grew and expanded. It has amazing chapters as well as painful ones. Stories of triumph and stories of great mistakes. But through it all Jesus walked with her and cared for her, and at every turn he *loved* her.

Today, people all over the world gather together in the name of Jesus. Thousands of languages lifting up his name week in and week out. We feed millions of people, write music, care for the poor, preach sermons, and plant more and more churches to express the heart of Jesus in every corner of the world.

This is *our* story. From one man who died a criminal's death on a cross to a world changed.

This is the movement of the church.

It is the greatest movement the world has ever seen.

Then why doesn't it feel like it?

We go to church on most weekends. We have great times and bad times. But if we were honest, we'd have to admit that sometimes we feel as though we're going through the motions. We have a confrontation with someone. We have a bad meeting with our pastor. We see imperfections in each other or our leadership up close and begin to lose heart. And we begin to think, *Maybe I'm on the losing team here. This is probably not the church for me. There are a few churches that still "get it"—maybe I need to go to one of those. Or maybe church in general is not for me. I have just been burned one too many times.*

If that's how you feel, you are not alone.

WHY YOU SHOULD KEEP READING

It doesn't matter what your church looks like. House church or megachurch. Whether you play folk music and have an artist painting while you preach or you sing hymns in a church with stained-glass windows. You are a part of the body of Christ. An amazing movement of God unlike anything the world has ever seen.

Maybe you have been struggling with your significance. Feeling like you are missing out on something great by sticking with your local church. You've seen all of its imperfections and are no longer enamored. Or maybe the media headlines and blog posts are starting to wear on you. Maybe you have had bad experiences with your church and are looking to move on. Maybe you already have.

This book is for you.

Every church is flawed. *Every* Christian is imperfect.

But God uses the messy and imperfect to make something beautiful. He chose the foolish and unqualified to confound the wise and change the world.

Something special happens when you dive headlong into a community of the imperfect and walk out the gospel of love in your local church. No amount of books, blogs, podcasts, or conferences can ever replace the spiritual growth that results from the hard work it takes to commit to a local church. And it isn't just to benefit us and our communities; this is something close to the heart of Jesus.

> You are a part of the body of Christ. An amazing movement of God unlike anything the world has ever seen.

The church is called the "body of Christ," and nothing is closer to someone than his or her body. We are called the "bride of Christ" because the relationship between a husband and wife is a sacred union. These are the words God uses to describe us. And no matter what her state, no matter what she looks like on the outside, Jesus loves and cares for her.

In the midst of the struggle of living out the local church, it's easy to forget the unbreakable love God has for us. Sometimes we get so caught up in our circumstances that we lose perspective.

THE NEXT BIG THING

There was a moment on our first tour when I walked out on stage in front of a crowd of 10,000 in St. Louis. And it was there that it hit me. Our dream had come true. After years of praying and dreaming, OUTCRY was off the ground. And our first year was incredible. Our tour traveled almost eight thousand miles to twelve cities. We had 130,000 in attendance our *first year,* and 10,000 were saved. Packed-out arenas in every city we went.

Not only that, but every night we had worship together *before* we began. Each evening before we hit the stage, a different group led worship. Hillsong United, Crowder, Kari Jobe, Jesus Culture, Passion, Bethel Music, Trip Lee, and Lauren Daigle all in the same room taking turns leading a devotional and worship. It was a room full of some of the most influential and creative worship leaders in the world (not to mention personal heroes of mine) having a small group together. A dream come true and in every sense of the word, special.

But the most exciting thing for me was the *reason* OUTCRY existed. We weren't just assembling amazing worship artists (though we were). We weren't just trying to get big crowds (though we were). Our heart from the beginning was for the movement greater than all movements put together. The movement that happens every week, in every city, in all corners of the world.

The local church.

OUTCRY is not the next "movement" to join. It is not the next big thing in the church. It is a symptom of what God is already doing. We are entering a season unlike anything we've seen in recent history, where churches and ministries are talking about working together and championing each other. Putting aside theological and political differences and showing the world a unified church. God is pulling us together in this season for a reason, and a new vision is emerging. But this new vision is actually not new at all. In the new, we will rediscover the ancient and immovable truth about the church.

As we dive in, keep an open mind. We have grown up (even in the church) talking about all of our past scars. We have consistently heard the idea that the church is ineffective, irrelevant, and dying.

But God's heart is not for us to be on the defensive.

This is the moment we shift the discussion from our imperfections and seek to see the church as Jesus

> God is pulling us together in this season for a reason, and a new vision is emerging. But this new vision is actually not new at all.

sees her: Forgiven. Adopted. Powerful. Imperfect carriers of a perfect love.

What you are about to read is a collection of thoughts, histories, philosophies, and stories with this one purpose: to remind you that the church is the greatest movement the world has ever seen. The part you play in your local church matters. You are an integral part of the amazing story of God that is unfolding all around us.

The next big thing is here. But it's been here for two thousand years. It's the local church.

[1]

DOES THE CHURCH STILL MATTER?

I feel at this juncture of our journey, introductions are in order. My name is Ryan Romeo. I came to know Jesus when I was fifteen years old through a young youth pastor—who is still one of my closest friends—named Joel Fritz. My life changed. Not only as I encountered Jesus but also through Joel's discipleship and the relationships I forged in that small church. Ever since that time in my life, I have spent significant time volunteering as well as serving on staff at local churches. My wife, Blake, and I have done missions work from Asia to South America and have seen the church in a form quite different than what we see and experience in the US. I've led worship, and I've been a graphic artist for different churches and musicians all over the country. I have a heart for Jesus and his church and share this passion with my good friend Shane Quick.

Now, Shane works with some of the biggest names in Christian music and—like me—has a heart to see the church championed and encouraged. He gets a mile-high view of the church often and has brought me along in seeing the people of God from a vantage point few get to see. *Combined,* he and I see a wide spectrum of the movement of God. From the small, struggling local body, to the international megachurch that influences millions of people, and everything in between, we've seen it.

But we are not what you would call the "old guard" of church proponents.

We met as young leaders in our twenties working on a conference in 2010 called Crowder's Fantastical Church Music Conference in Waco, Texas. It was packed with some amazing artists and speakers, including Louie Giglio, Matt Redman, Francis Chan, the David Crowder*Band, Hillsong London, Jars of Clay, Leeland, Gungor, Rob Bell, The Civil Wars, John Mark McMillan, and many more. Behind the scenes the conference was truly something special. Some of the world's most creative and influential leaders in the church, all in one place. We both experienced something that only someone like Crowder could pull together. It was an amazing variety of speakers and musicians that made a deep impression on me and Shane. We saw the beautiful and unexpected diversity of this amazing movement called the church.

After that, Shane and I went our separate ways. I continued to work at a church in Tucson, Arizona. I was also bi-vocational at the time and filled the rest of my salary at my dad's business doing manufacturing. I loved working with my dad and learned a ton, but it felt like it was a step away from the dreams God had placed in me. On top of that, my wife and I were expecting our second child. And just when I felt God was settling me in that place—just when I started to feel like the passion he had instilled in me was beginning to wane—my phone rang. It was Shane.

We began talking about a potential conference called OUTCRY. We talked for a couple of hours about what we would say at this conference. And the entire time we were talking, our focus was not on musicians or new trends but on the oldest movement we knew: the local church.

At the end of the conversation he said he had just started working with a group called Jesus Culture and that I should come out to LA to hang out and dream some more. And so the process of dreaming about OUTCRY began. Shane would call . . . I would fly somewhere . . . we would talk and dream . . . then I would return home.

Call. Fly. Dream. Repeat.

The more we met, the more we began to see that we didn't carry the usual millennial narrative of wanting to see the church drastically change to look more like us. We didn't see a dying church. We didn't see a church struggling for relevance. We spoke from both a higher vantage point—the church from thirty-nine thousand feet—and in a close and personal way, discussing the pastors who had changed our lives. We didn't talk about what the church *should* or *could* be doing—we talked about the identity that the church carries and the impact it has on us. We felt reactionary against all of the judgment—external *and internal*—that we as young leaders were expected to carry.

This was the beginning of the message we rolled out with OUTCRY. There is still hope in the past, present, and future of the church. In the church, our best days are ahead.

But why doesn't it feel like it? Looking around, it's hard to find people with a hopeful outlook on the church or its future.

A SEASON OF CRITIQUE

All around us people are sharing the ills and imperfections of the church. We read viral blogs telling us how we are "missing it" with millennials or how we have become increasingly irrelevant in society. We read headlines about the demise of the church and how if we don't adapt to the changing tide of society, we will die. Not only do they *say* this, but they come prepared with polling data! Much of this data stems from a study by the American Religious Identification Survey[1] (ARIS), which noted several statistics about the church. It showed that from 1990 to 2009 people who self-identified as "Christian" fell from 86 to 76 percent. This prompted the infamous headline from *Newsweek* magazine that year titled "The End of Christian America."[2] And the diagnosis from the media isn't slowing down.

> There is still hope in the past, present, and future of the church. In the church, our best days are ahead.

CNN ran a headline on its website stating "Millennials leaving church in droves, study finds."[3] In the article the author states, "It's not just millennials leaving the church. Whether married or single, rich or poor, young or old, living in the West or the Bible Belt, almost every demographic group has seen a significant drop in people who call them-selves Christians, Pew found." That Pew[4] study showed that between 2007 and 2014, self-described Evangelical Christians fell in the US by 0.9 percent while people who described their religious identity as "Unaffiliated" rose by 6.7 percent. Recently, the *Huffington Post* introduced an article on Christianity by saying, "The numbers may vary but the trend line is consistent: The Christian church is in decline. From church attendance to those who identify as Christian, all numbers are heading south."[5]

All numbers are heading south.

Like a tidal wave of public opinion, the narrative of a failing church is growing stronger. All around us, the data shows a struggling, dying church. To people outside the church, there seem to be a faithful few hanging on to a dying movement. A group of out of touch, stuck in the past, fuddy-duddies sitting in uncomfortable pews, drink-ing bad coffee, and totally ignoring an inevitable demise!

That may be a bit dramatic. But it isn't that far off from the prevailing view of the church.

And I wish I could say this is just an outsider's perspec-tive. Unfortunately it's not. In fact, a lot from the critique we see comes from *inside* the church.

Recently there have been many viral blogs hitting social media about all the problems with the church. We hear advice from well-meaning (I assume) Christians on how to better reach millennials, or what we really need to do to *accurately* follow the teachings of Jesus. Loads of unsolicited advice for those of us remaining in our local church. We have influential pastors telling us to be more relevant to society. Whether talking theology, politics, or style of service, we know how to rip each other apart for all the world to see. We casually throw out lines like, "The church has largely failed at . . ." or "The church is terrible at . . ." Just fill in the blank.

But is all of this critique bad? Shouldn't we confront areas in which the church needs to improve? After all, how can we get better at what we do if we don't have those inside critiquing? I mean, at some point we need to confront some of this stuff, right?

I couldn't agree more.

But at what point does the critique cease to be productive? Does painting each other in broad strokes produce the fruit we think it does?

This generation tends to believe that our perception is reality. If we *feel* like the church is dying *and* all the stats show that it's in decline, then it must be true.

But is it? *Is* perception reality when it comes to the church?

As a defense against the critique, many Christians

have opted to leave the flawed institution of the church and pursue God on their own terms. Without all the difficulty and inconvenience of working with different generations, political beliefs, or different views on theology. Many have decided to fashion their own, custom church life.

I'LL JUST STAY HOME

Early in my experience as a worship leader I had a pastor who saw through my immaturity and inexperience and actually hired me. He was the first leader to believe in me. My wife and I committed to him and his ministry and quickly found ourselves in a community of people we loved. We started a small group of young married couples, genuinely living our lives together and seeing God move in awesome ways.

But a few years in we were blindsided by the announcement that the leader—whom I loved and looked up to—was moving to another town. He was dealing with a lot of circumstances outside of his control, and I didn't blame him at all. I was and am still so impacted by his influence in my life. But once he left, we quickly found ourselves holding the pieces of a local church in crisis.

We had about one hundred people stick it out as we began to look for a pastor. I was leading worship every week, leading our small group, and preaching occasionally. My wife and I were pouring our hearts and souls into the place week after week. Month after month.

Then one day we found him. A young preacher with a gift for leading and preaching. We liked him, he liked us, and he seemed to fit the bill. After prayerfully walking through the interview process, we hired him. But soon I realized that this guy was a motivated, driven leader coming into our church fresh and ready to go. I was not. I am a very driven leader, but by this point I had nearly driven myself into the ground. And a few heated meetings later, I knew I had to move on.

It was heartbreaking.

As we stepped away from our community, we felt isolated and lonely. Burned. I felt the refreshment of just going to a coffee shop on Sunday and not having to *lead* anyone. No drama. No bad church coffee. I felt free.

We still got together with our small group. We had some worship and taught each other. Many of them also left the church by this point and were feeling quite satisfied doing a small group but not attending a church. We were in community. Worshipping God. We were serving the neighborhood. I mean, what were we missing by not attending a church?

But Blake and I knew we were missing something.

I genuinely have nothing against the house church movement. On the contrary, I love it. It is a beautiful thing to live in community with others in such a deep way. In a home is where genuine bonds are forged and where we get the opportunity to exercise the gifts God has given us. House churches are a meaningful and beautiful expression of the church.

But there is also something to be said for a large, diverse group of people coming together every week. A group of different people, in the same city, of all generations, trying their best to follow Jesus and love one another. There is a growth and connection that comes when the people of God commit to one another. Through all of the messiness and imperfection.

The years since, my wife and I have had different opportunities that moved us to different churches. We have been led to new churches and new seasons of life. But through it all, we always committed to pouring our heart into the local church. Committing to the local body in front of us no matter how big or small it was.

Committing to a local church changed my life. It wasn't the perfection of those around me, or the same-mindedness that produced fruit. It wasn't the style of worship or the quality of the preaching. It was working with those who thought differently than myself. Those from different generations and social backgrounds. As it says in Proverbs, it was the "iron sharpens iron" situations that brought lasting impact to my life.

And when you commit, there are often times of tension. Times that don't *feel* significant or particularly spiritual. But the tensions we so often run away from can be the very thing God uses to bring the maturity and opportunity we are looking for.

THE CHURCHLESS CHRISTIAN

Our society leans toward the idea that self-sufficiency is greater than relying on others. The idea that we don't really *need* others to live a full life. We consider the difficulties and inconvenience of community something that gets in the way of a happy and fulfilled life. Often we are encouraged to remove ourselves from difficult or frustrating relationships to maintain a happy, stress-free life. And this idea has seeped into the church.

There is no shortage of books or articles talking about the burned-out Christians who leave the institution of the church and blaze out on their own to follow Jesus in the way that seems best to them. They seek an environment free from all of the distractions and inconveniences of interacting with all of the frustrating people in their local church.

So, is staying at home the way to combat the perception of the church? Is simply pouring into your *personal* relationship with God and leaving the difficult situations at a local church the answer?

A personal walk with God is very important *and* biblical. God often speaks to individuals and guides them on unique paths with unique gifts. But God is also a corporate God, and he speaks to the group as well as the individual.

Most of the letters of the New Testament were written to *churches*—communities that had their own struggles and issues to work through. They were diverse groups of people that needed to learn corporately as well as individually during the time before printed, canonized Scripture. They had no Bibles for their personal quiet times or small Bible studies. On top of that, most of the people were illiterate, so they relied on a select few to read letters from Paul or John. Every step of the church was taken with deep reliance on one another. The idea that they were self-sufficient in their walk with God would have been alien at best.

We have more resources available to us than any other time in history. We have Bibles, books, magazines, podcasts, blogs, and more. We can fashion our own church experience using the music we like and the theologies we agree with. And if we hear anything we don't like, we can just turn it off!

But ultimately God created the church for a purpose. He created community for a purpose. From the story of Adam and Eve we see that we were created to be in community with others. No amount of blogs or podcasts can produce the same impact on your life as committing to your local church.

That's why OUTCRY began. We want you who are involved in the church to commit to your local congregation. The here and now. We want you to embrace the church and community in front of you. To pour yourself into the friends and leaders that *know your name*. To commit to the local expression of the global movement of Jesus, knowing that it is imperfect. But it's this local commitment that—when multiplied—transforms the world around us.

UNITED AND DIVERSE

There are many ways the Bible talks about the church. It's full of beautiful allegory on this subject. I love how Paul in 1 Corinthians 12 refers to the church as the "body of Christ" (v. 27). You cannot get closer to someone than their *body*. It shows the oneness and special connection Jesus has with his church is unlike any other connection.

There is also diversity in the body—a diversity that is meant to remain, not to be flattened or blended.

I want you to think about how all this makes you more significant, not less. A body isn't just a single part blown up into something huge. It's all the different-but-similar parts arranged and functioning together. If Foot said, "I'm not elegant like Hand, embellished with rings; I guess I don't belong to this body," would that make it so? If Ear said, "I'm not beautiful like Eye, limpid and expressive; I don't deserve a place on the head," would you want to remove it from the body? If the body was all eye, how could it hear? If all ear, how could it smell? As it is, we see that God has carefully placed each part of the body right where he wanted it. (1 Corinthians 12:14–18 MSG)

In most scenarios, the larger an *organization* gets the less significant *you* become. You sit in increasingly smaller cubicles. You receive more and more specific job descriptions. Their reliance on you shrinks and, in turn, your passion for the job decreases. It is easy to feel like another face in the crowd. Another easily replaced cog in the machine. But this isn't so in Jesus's kingdom.

In the kingdom of God, the sum of all the parts is what makes the sum so beautiful. The one who designed you and built you puts you in a specific place in his organization. And the mystery is this: no matter how large and complicated his movement gets, your significance never shrinks.

God never does anything without purpose. Without a destiny in mind. He hasn't placed you haphazardly into the church you serve. He has carefully and deliberately placed you where he wants you. He has carefully and purposefully filled your church with the people he intended to.

And beyond this, each *church* carries great significance. The church of fifty-five people meeting in a small, steepled building in a Midwestern town carries the same significance as the megachurch in a major city. In the body of Christ, each community of believers is unique and built for a specific purpose in the greater movement of Jesus. And in God's economy, the hierarchy of significance is leveled. Not every church makes the same *impact* when it comes to numbers, but every church carries the same *significance* when dealing with individual lives.

> Not every church makes the same *impact*, but every church carries the same *significance*.

THE LOCAL MOVEMENT

Everything is going local. From produce to craft beers, western society is gravitating toward a local representation in everything it consumes. Some of the top documentaries on Netflix center around local food or how unhealthy large-scale food production is. There are new trends in homes that are smaller than two hundred square feet, and more and more people are choosing to ride a bicycle to work. Local. Small. Around-the-corner living.

There is this insatiable hunger emerging in our culture for the local. The tangible. The right-here-and-now. Not viewing the world through a screen, but being face to face with one another. The feeling of being a part of a tight community of people who taste, see, and hear the world around them uniquely. Experiencing something that no one else on earth can experience unless they are in *your* city. *Your* town. *Your* neighborhood.

The church is the original *local* movement. The first movement that had a *global* identity with *local* expressions. And this is the beauty and strength of the church today.

We don't all look the same. Maybe you are in a thriving house church. Maybe you attend a megachurch. Chances are, you are somewhere in between. No matter what your church looks like, it is hugely significant. And not in terms of numbers. In terms of the kingdom. In terms of *the body*.

The strength of the local church is that there are many facets of God represented. Each local congregation embodies a specific culture and uniquely represents God in that culture. Paul refers to this as the *manifold* wisdom of God. A kaleidoscope of God's attributes shown through the diversity and uniqueness of all the local churches combined.

We've seen this at OUTCRY. From each artist—Hillsong United to Crowder to Kari Jobe to Trip Lee—we saw a multifaceted display of the church. Different leaders and styles converging on one stage. But further than that, churches from all over the country uniting together to worship Jesus and encourage his bride. A beautiful display of what God is doing all around the world in this season.

DEEPER THAN WE CAN SEE

In John 13:34–35 Jesus tells us that we are a light and that "the world"—those on the outside—would see our light and know about him by how we love each other. But in Ephesians 3 we find out that not only are we a light to the *world* in our unity, but we—now this is totally nuts—show the *angels* ("authorities in the heavenly realms") the multifaceted wisdom of God. *We* actually reveal more perspective on the wisdom of God *to* the angels! We carry more authority and significance in the kingdom than what we can see in *this* world.

> His intent was that now, through the church, the manifold wisdom of God should be made known to the rulers and authorities in the heavenly realms. (Ephesians 3:10)

Imagine you come across an ancient tree in the forest. It has a rough exterior. Gnarled branches. It looks old. It smells old. On the outside it looks dead. Dry, rough, and grey. Lifeless. But beneath the rough exterior there is life. Through to the tree's core there are rings in the wood signifying all of its ancient history. Under the ground there is a labyrinth and tangle of roots that go far deeper than you can see. There is a hidden strength, depth, and beauty that is beyond what you experience on the outside.

This is the church. There is power and significance in the local church. We may not *feel* it. We may not *see* it or hear about it. But it is there. The local church is the greatest movement the world has ever seen, and you and I are at the center of it.

It's easy to be discouraged about polls and opinions. It's easy to be swayed by the words around us into believing that the church is dying and irrelevant. But that *perspective* does not line up with God's *reality*. There is a significance and greatness in the church that doesn't come from its numbers. Or its political influence. Or cultural relevance. No amount of blog articles, podcasts, or books can diminish the greatness of the local church because that greatness is bestowed to us straight from heaven. And it is irrevocable.

THROUGH HIS EYES

We were a couple months away from introducing the world to OUTCRY, and Shane and I were in Redding, California, working on our first promo video. We had been working on it for weeks. Trying to pour our heart and vision for the tour into a promo video less than two minutes long. It was not easy. And as we sat to review our first draft, we all realized the video wasn't right. The copy for the voiceover needed to be redone, and we were quickly running out of time. Not good. It was a responsibility that weighed on my shoulders, and I was feeling the pressure.

But as I went back to my hotel and began to write, I felt a surge of creativity and began to furiously type word after word. Suddenly I wrote a line that stopped me in my tracks. It was bold and so contrary to what I've been told that I knew it must be from God. It made me feel hesitant to write the words, but as I did it awakened a deep sense of excitement in me. As if I had written something that carried an ancient and hidden truth. Not based on what I experienced on the *outside* but what I knew to be true on the *inside*.

She is not dying.
She is not in decline.
Her best days are ahead.

Something about that moment seemed prophetic to me.

As I wrote those words, I could hear the realist in me say, "Ryan, she is in decline! Haven't you read all of the stats about the exodus of people from the local church? Don't stick your head in the sand! You have to confront reality!"

But in that moment, I felt something shift in me. In my perspective. I was not seeing the church through my own eyes. I began to see the church as Jesus sees her: loved, forgiven, diverse, messy yet beautiful. And contrary to what we've been told, she is around to stay.

After this I began to feel more offended by the viral blog posts telling us of all the problems with the church and offering solutions. I began to feel like a man hearing rumors about his bride-to-be and knowing they weren't at all true. Like divine gossip about the bride of Jesus. And I found myself thinking as I read these blogs, *Be careful what you say about the bride of Christ! Don't you know that Jesus loves her? Don't you know he died for her?*

We are not reverent toward the church, mostly because we weren't raised by a generation that was. But I believe we need more reverence when we talk about her. When we criticize "the church," we need to remember that it is made up of billions of different people. The earth is filled with different congregations in different communities, and criticism is not one-size-fits-all. The church is Jesus's bride. When we talk about her we talk about him.

YOU DON'T KNOW HER AS I DO

My wife, Blake, is incredible. She is amazingly supportive and loving—even in difficult seasons when I'm on the road. The thing about Blake is that she has an amazing depth to her. She doesn't preach sermons or try to dump biblical wisdom on anyone who will listen. But she wakes up every morning at five (when I'm usually snoring) and reads the Bible and prays. Then when I think we are going to have a normal conversation, she amazes me with moments of godly depth and insight.

If you only had a cursory relationship with her, you may never experience that side of Blake. I do, because I *know* her and have walked through life with her since the seventh grade—I know, pause and say, "Aaawe!"

Now, let's say we are good friends but you hated my wife. Under these circumstances we could have a relationship, but it would be strained. We would continually tiptoe around her in our conversations. We would hold each other at arm's length and ultimately never have a healthy relationship. You and I would both know that you hated something very special to me, and that would cause an undeniable tension. You can't love me but tell others blanket statements about her. Gossip about her around town when you don't know the depths of her personality. You don't know her as I do. Ultimately, you can't love me and hate my wife.

You can't love Jesus and hate his bride.

SHANE QUICK
OUTCRY

THE ROOTS

OUTCRY began when the pastor at my local church in Cullman, Alabama, asked me to start a college group. We had a very average-sized church of around 250 people, and Cullman isn't exactly a college town. We had about 6 to 8 college students but no college leader. I said yes but suggested we make it a group that could meet in someone's home. So a very energetic woman named Vicky, who had a heart for young people and was very special to me and my wife, Kim, said she would open up her home for our group to meet in every Tuesday night.

When we got together that very first night, right from the very start, God began to do something in the hearts of the students who came out. We simply worshiped, prayed, and encouraged one another. The first study we went through was the book *Twelve Ordinary Men* by

John MacArthur. We dove into who the disciples were before Jesus and who they became after they encountered Jesus. It was very powerful for us as a group.

One night a student approached me and asked if I would be okay with another group of students from another church joining us. And I said, "Of course! Please invite them!" And this was one of the tipping points for our group. It was one of the things that broke it all loose.

Word began to spread that this group was open to all churches. So even more came. And during our first month we saw eight churches come together, and it grew to more than fifty people. At this point Vicky told me she had no more room for the large number of people. So we began to look for a new space in which to meet. Somewhere neutral. So we moved to a basement in the local Colonel Cullman Museum, which the fire marshal said would fit one hundred people.

The night we moved locations, we immediately hit capacity. Worship was amazing. We dove into the life and calling of Jesus. We had pastors and youth pastors there who were being refreshed and encouraged. There was a real sense of unity in the room that was unbelievably powerful. No agendas. No promotion. Just lifting up the name of Jesus and asking what he wanted in our lives and community.

We stayed there for about a month before we moved to an old gymnasium. Soon we began seeing 250 to 300 people come every night. With summer approaching, however, we were afraid that students would leave and attendance would drop. But—on the contrary—we saw an amazing jump in attendance, and by the end of the summer, with our numbers having grown to 900, we had to change locations again. Each night we worshipped passionately. Every night we saw people saved.

One thing we did each night was speak to senior pastors and youth pastors, encouraging them and speaking life into them. And from that a culture of family and camaraderie emerged, which began to change the church community and our city. At the end of our first year we had grown to the point that nationally known worship leaders were traveling to Cullman for our events.

One night—on the biggest night we had ever had—God spoke to me. It was as clear as day that he wanted that night to be our last night. But with this directive came an assurance from him that it would come back someday in a different form. Now, by this time we had around fifty leaders who were really making these nights happen. Some of these leaders, who had been with us since the original Bible study, had now taken over these amazing nights. When I met with them and told them what God was saying, it was devastating to them. But we held on to the promise that OUTCRY would come back in a new way. In a new form. That our heart and passion for God and unity in his church would return through OUTCRY again.

As the years went by, I developed relationships with some of the most influential worship and church leaders in the world. From Hillsong to Kari Jobe to Jesus Culture, God began opening doors I never imagined would be opened. And by the time the OUTCRY tour began in 2015, God had taken what began as a small Bible study and resurrected it into the force that it is today. And our heart continues to beat for worship, the gospel, and lifting up the greatest movement in all of history—the local church.

[2]

CAN WE BE PROUD OF THE CHURCH?

grew up in Tucson, Arizona, which is not exactly the Bible Belt. Tucson has one of the most unchurched populations in the nation and is not very friendly to Christians. I lived most of my first fifteen years hearing very little about Jesus or the church. And what I *did* hear did not leave a good impression. I heard of all the past transgressions of the church and felt no need to dive further. I knew that the church was filled with hypocrites and had a very troubled past. And that was it for me.

I don't believe I'm the only one to experience the church or its history like that.

If you ask the average college student at a major university about church history, he or she may say something like, "Well, there were the Crusades, right? Cutting people's heads off who didn't join the church. And . . . weren't there some witch trials in Salem? People burned at the stake? . . . . And I remember something about a guy named Luther nailing paper to a door."

The *Reader's Digest* version of church history that most of us in the West receive is small and mostly negative. As Christians we know all of the mistakes and begin to feel the church is, ultimately, not something to be proud of. It's something to apologize for and tiptoe around. Maybe we have a sense that it is so flawed and embarrassing that we need to distance ourselves and make up for it by being a "better" church.

And what would be so bad about that? Shouldn't we improve from the past? Move forward?

But what if we are missing information? What if the history of the church had amazing moments to be proud of? Then we may be missing out. Missing out on the pride of being a part of a movement with a great and rich heritage. Missing out on honoring the past and stepping on the shoulders of giants to reach greater heights.

I spent some time with my friend Luke Parker talking about church history. Luke's father directs the local Fuller

Theological Seminary campus in Phoenix, and both of his parents are brilliant pastors. His upbringing was saturated in theology and church. He is one of the smartest guys I know, and when he says, "In the original language the Bible says . . ." I *know* he has actually read and understood the original language. This is Luke.

One day I was picking his brain about church history, and he began to share some things I found very surprising. I knew deep down that there were great moments in the church that I was unaware of, but as we talked, I found my horizons broadening. My *vision* of the movement that I am a part of—the local church—began to zoom back, and I gained some perspective. Some pride.

Let's look at some snapshots of the history of our movement—the other side of the story. Not a whitewashed history, but high points for us to look at with pride. We are all aware of the failings of the church, but as you read, allow pride to swell. Allow passion to rise up in the imperfect but beautiful story of *us*.

THE UNLIKELY START TO A WORLDWIDE MOVEMENT

Let's say you wanted to start something. Something big. Not hundreds of people. Not thousands of people. Not even millions. We're talking *billions* of people. A movement. A revolution that would spread in every language to all corners of the world. And to accomplish this you had *endless* resources. We're talking never-emptying bank accounts. Extensive databases of people and contacts. Cell phone numbers of all the movers and shakers around the world. If that weren't enough, you can actually control time. You can take however much time you need to get this thing off the ground. You can start this movement at any point in history. The past and future are at your fingertips! So how would you start? What strategy would you take?

I think most of us would hire the best people. Put together extensive plans. Marketing strategies would be laid out. Board rooms would be full of suits and catered lunches. Private jets would be rushing the globe for meetings between political who's who. You may begin writing books, producing TV commercials, and putting together social media campaigns. Thousands mobilized. Billions of dollars spent. Every resource utilized until the world heard the news of this movement. Logos pasted from Times Square to a children's soccer field in Kenya.

Most of us would approach it this way. It makes sense. Unload all you can think of to spread the word, and don't stop until it happens.

But somehow God passed on this brilliant strategy. In fact, he did the opposite.

He chose to start two thousand years ago. He came in a time with no social media. No cell phones. No cars or planes. The printing press wasn't even invented. There was literally no way to get the word out other than by *talking* to people or handwriting them a note. Not exactly the best time to come for worldwide communications.

He came through a teen mom. Through an impoverished family. Born in a dirty manger. He grew up working with his hands. He was not in society's inner circle. He was not well connected or networked with the elites of the day. Not exactly the social structure you'd want to be dropped into.

Not only that, but after growing up in this inopportune time, he chose to give himself three years to launch his movement. Three years! And in those three short years, he chose to lead twelve very unremarkable people—whom we'll discuss later. Then he willingly died in front of them. A brutal death reserved for criminals. There's a leadership curveball for you. Not a strategy I'd employ in starting *my* movement.

After this, his beaten-down and confused disciples scattered.

But then he came back to life! The movement was *literally* resurrected. His disciples were amazed and overjoyed to see their friend and leader return. Now *this* was a good idea! Get their attention, and then lead the movement to success. But what did he do then? His last words to his followers were:

> "Go and make disciples of all nations, baptizing them in the name of the Father and of the Son and of the Holy Spirit, and teaching them to obey everything I have commanded you. And surely I am with you always, to the very end of the age." (Matthew 28:19–20)

> "Alright guys I'm outta here. But make sure to tell and train everyone on earth to obey the commandments I never wrote down for you. Hopefully a few of you took notes. But don't worry! I know you are watching me leave you, but I'll be right here," he adds as he taps his fist to his chest. (The Official Ryan Romeo Translation)

Then he left. He flew away, leaving his disciples befuddled, standing and staring into the sky. And they were to take this message to "all nations" when they had no way of traveling the world. He left them with an *impossible* task.

This is not the way to start a movement.

The church began with a man whose trust in God was so deep and profound that he employed no earthly logic to start it. He could have walked with the disciples for decades and slowly transferred leadership to them as they learned the ropes and earned their place. He could have written books and hosted luncheons. But he didn't.

> Our movement began on the foundation of the miraculous. God built a scenario that was literally impossible to conquer, and he conquered it.

Our movement began on the foundation of the miraculous. God built a scenario that was literally impossible to conquer, and he conquered it. In a small, dirty, violent corner of the world his movement started. With no fanfare he began his movement in the most unlikely of times. For all intents and purposes, it should *not* have worked. But amazingly enough, it did. And this is just the beginning of our story.

THE SEED OF GROWTH

The early years of the church were marked by fierce and violent opposition. In Acts we meet a man named

Stephen. He was chosen by the disciples to "wait on tables" so that the disciples could do ministry. Stephen was a servant, "a man full of God's grace and power, [who] performed great wonders and signs among the people" (6:8). This is the kind of guy you want on your team. He served others and was known for being full of God's grace and power.

But his good reputation hit the ears of the religious leaders, and Stephen found himself in hot water. They dragged him into their courtroom and drilled him. He responded by preaching Jesus boldly. Albeit, he didn't have the most sensitive wrap-up, but what happened next sparked a reaction that still reverberates throughout the entire history of the church. Stephen was brutally killed. Stoned, in fact. He was the first martyr for Jesus. And the Bible says, "On that day a great persecution broke out against the church in Jerusalem" (8:1).

Great persecution.

If you want to squash a movement, start killing all of its leaders with large stones in the middle of the street. I mean, who in their right mind would die like that for a new philosophy. For a message they had *just* heard.

To reinforce this point, there were other movements beginning at the time that had been destroyed by persecution. Earlier in Acts we meet a Pharisee named

Gamaliel who spoke about the effect persecution had on other movements at the time. And it didn't exactly *grow* them.

> Men of Israel, consider carefully what you intend to do to these men. Some time ago Theudas appeared, claiming to be somebody, and about four hundred men rallied to him. He was killed, all his followers were dispersed, and it all came to nothing. After him, Judas the Galilean appeared in the days of the census and led a band of people in revolt. He too was killed, and all his followers were scattered. Therefore, in the present case I advise you: Leave these men alone! Let them go! For if their purpose or activity is of human origin, it will fail. But if it is from God, you will not be able to stop these men; you will only find yourselves fighting against God. (Acts 3:35–39)

Several other movements at the time were destroyed by persecution. A revolutionary leader would emerge, the powers-that-be would step in and kill the leader and persecute his followers, then it would all fall apart. The death of a revolutionary leader and the persecution of his followers would always kill the movement. It was a proven method. But not *our* movement. The movement of Jesus inexplicably grows under persecution. In fact, it seems to even *promote* growth. When things get tough, we find encouragement in the Bible to keep going.

> We are hard pressed on every side, but not crushed; perplexed, but not in despair; persecuted, but not abandoned; struck down, but not destroyed. (2 Corinthians 4:8–9)

Christian writer Tertullian wrote in the second century that "the blood of martyrs is the seed of the church." One major reason for growth in the church is seeing those around you killed for believing in the same thing as you. Time and again we see that God takes the logical and rational approach to growing his movement and does *the opposite*.

CARING FOR THE SICK

Have you noticed that there is a common theme in the hospitals you see? Look around and pay attention to some of the names. Many hospitals carry the name "St. Mary's" or "St. Joseph's." This isn't a coincidence. The church has always been about caring for the sick and dying.

Heal the sick, raise the dead, cleanse those who
have leprosy, drive out demons. Freely you have
received; freely give. (Matthew 10:8)

In the verse above, Jesus tells his disciples to heal
the sick, and this is something the church has always
taken seriously. It wasn't only made manifest through
the miraculous—though that is clearly what Jesus did.
Throughout its history, the church has been right in the
middle of science and technology. It has pursued knowing more about the machine known as the human body
and has sought to *heal the sick*. We have had this in our
DNA from the very beginning.

A plague broke out in third-century Rome. It was
not an ordinary sort of disease; this one wiped out thousands. By some accounts it killed as many as two-thirds
of the population of Alexandria. It was the sort of thing
that affected everyone. Death, disease, and fear were
everywhere you went. The Christian leader Dionysius
wrote about it to the people in Alexandria and said, "In
these days there are lamentations everywhere, and all are
mourning: wailings resound through the city by reason
of the number of the dead and the dying day by day."[6]
In that time, it would have been a truly terrifying and

devastating thing you would have literally "avoided like the plague."

But not us. Not our movement. When everyone was running from this disease, we were flooding in to care for them. This wasn't because Christians thought that they were miraculously immune, either. Many of them died as they sought to care for those dying. Even in the burial of the bodies, Christians risked their lives. Dionysius continued in his letter to compare how the church responded counter to the rest of the culture:

> Taking up the bodies of the saints on their arms and breasts, closing their eyes and shutting their mouths, bearing them on their shoulders and laying them out for burial, clinging to them, embracing them, washing them, decking them out, they not long after had the same services rendered to them; for many of the survivors followed in their train. But the Gentiles behaved quite differently: those who were beginning to fall sick they thrust away, and their dearest they fled from, or cast them half dead into the roads: unburied bodies they treated as vile refuse.

Ancient Rome, Medieval Europe, and early America

didn't have a standard welfare system. If you lived in that time, your retirement plan was not your 401(k)—it was your children. Your insurance was not a business or the government. If you were badly sick or if you were permanently injured, there was no agency that would rescue you. But then the church stepped in. We built hospitals run by churches and monasteries, many of which offered free healthcare to those who could not afford it.

This is what we do. We care for the sick. Even when it puts us at risk, our movement *heals the sick* just as Jesus commanded. And as we do that, we affect culture. Healthcare and a value for the sick is so engrained in our Western society that it's hard to remember where it came from. The church is that force humming in the background of history. Overlooked by many but affecting everyone. A sound that's hard to perceive at first but gets louder and louder once you hone in on it.

> The church is that force humming in the background of history. Overlooked by many but affecting everyone.

Healthcare is not the only cultural phenomenon that finds much of its roots in the church. The church had major influence in a place in history that may be surprising to many people today: art.

STUDYING ART

I graduated with a degree in fine arts from the University of Arizona. It isn't exactly a normal prerequisite for church ministry. Art school is quite different than seminary. It wouldn't be considered a bastion of Christian thought and philosophy. In fact, most of the students and professors have a very tainted view of the church.

But as I studied among a culture so opposed to Christianity, something unexpected happened. It was in art history that I found the rich and beautiful heritage of the church. I found myself smiling and looking around the class thinking, *Don't you guys see what we are studying here?*

Much of the art we know and study today had its roots in the church. While working at a conference, I met W. David O. Taylor, who really opened my eyes on this subject. In his book *For the Beauty of the Church: Casting a Vision for the Arts* he shows that the church has historically been the creative and even financial force behind art. Not only did we say we supported artists, but we actually paid their bills. Yes, the church *funded* artists, from Michelangelo to Rembrandt. The movements of Gothic, Renascence, and Rococo were funded by the church and are now studied in art school.

You begin to see that a majority of art—from paintings

to architecture to music—all began with a desire to display the beauty of God. This was a tangible expression of the artists' honor and worship to our creator. We pushed boundaries in displaying the beauty of the human body or the meaning behind an architectural feature. We explored the world around us and created our own artistic expressions.

Look at architecture alone. The truth is that just about any architecture built between the fall of the Roman empire and the 1800s has a significant connection to the Christian faith. Stained glass was used to tell biblical stories and show the beauty of creation through light. Ornate curved spires were created to lift your mind and heart to God. Many of the people in the towns of the time had been living in cramped, dirty conditions. But as they approached the churches, their eyes would be lifted to a different, more beautiful place. The goal of architecture of that time was to lift your mind to heaven.

I love how the church was not simply a passive observer of the arts but integral in creating new art and culture.

I don't believe our place in the arts is over. Just look at the art coming out of the church now. From music to video, the church is beginning to push the boundaries of creativity further and further. We are in one of the most creative moments in the history of the church. It may not feel like it, but nothing ever feels special when you are in the middle of it.

Keep an eye on church art. The next chapter of art history is being written, and I believe the church will increasingly be at the center of it.

HISTORY, EDUCATION, AND BEER

Imagine you lived in a time where you knew less than your father did about the world around you, and he knew less than his father. On top of that, the reality was that your children would know even less than you did. These were the Dark Ages. Knowledge was being sucked up and lost from generation to generation. A society defined by the dark, hopeless feeling of seeing culture and history lost. But it is always in the darkest periods in history that the light of the church shines brighter.

> It is always in the darkest periods in history that the light of the church shines brighter.

During the Dark Ages, monasteries became one of the few places to protect culture and history. They taught people to read and write. Before Gutenberg's printing press, monasteries were places of great discipline in copying biblical texts by hand. They not only protected sacred scriptures, but they kept other Greek manuscripts in tact as well. From Greek philosophy to mathematics, the church kept it all alive in those dark times. Out of these dark times universities were born. Justo Gonzalez wrote in his book *The Story of Christianity*,

> Universities were in part the result of the growth of cities. Students congregated in urban centers, *first at the cathedral schools* and then at others . . . Out of these evolved the main universities of Europe. The oldest universities in western Europe date from the late years of the twelfth century; but it was the thirteenth that witnessed the growth of universities as the main centers of study. Those who wished to study medicine [among other things] . . . [went to universities].

At every turn, the church kept the manuscripts of culture and history intact. Art, science, and philosophy kept alive by the church. But there is something else the church had its hand in that may surprise contemporary Christians: beer. Recently NPR published an article about beer and the church that stated,

As far back as the 18th century, Paulaner monks in Germany would brew and drink a heavy, malty type of beer called Doppelbock for Lent. The Paulaner monks weren't allowed to eat solid food for the duration of Lent, so the next best thing? Beer. The beer was so nutritious that it kept them nourished for the entire 40-day fast. The Paulaner Brewery in Munich still brews the Doppelbock beer today.[7]

Even Arthur Guinness himself was a Christian who brewed Guinness as an alternative to liquor to reduce drunkenness!

Despite what we hear, the movement of the local church historically cannot be broadly painted as anti-art or anti-science. We are purveyors of art, science, and culture unlike anything else in human history. From universities to beer, we have a rich history that is anything but boring.

HUMAN RIGHTS

When it comes to the subject of human rights, the church has had its share of tarnish throughout history. From slavery to child labor to women's rights, the church clearly has an imperfect past. At times Christians were willfully ignorant of these practices, but at other times they were active supporters. Still, at other times the church was on the *right* side of history with these subjects. The past is littered with Jesus followers who could see past the culture of their time and stand against these injustices. But before Abraham Lincoln or Martin Luther King Jr. there was a Christian revolutionary named William Wilberforce.

William Wilberforce is most known—though not known enough—as an abolitionist who was born in the mid-1700s in England. But Wilberforce didn't just lead the fight against slavery as a concerned citizen. As an adult, he became a Christian and began seeing injustices all around him. It wasn't simply that he hated slavery—though he did—it was his ability to imagine a society that cared for people in the same way God cared for people that enabled him to fight the institution. He dared to see the culture as it was and envision a new reality, a reality in which human rights took a central place in the political and cultural world around him.

Eric Metaxas wrote about the bravery and Christian roots of Wilberforce in his book *Amazing Grace: William Wilberforce and the Heroic Campaign to End Slavery.*

There's hardly a soul alive today who isn't horrified and offended by the very idea of human slavery. We seethe with moral indignation at it, and we can't fathom how anyone or any culture ever countenanced it. But in the world into which Wilberforce was born, the opposite was true . . . Everywhere on the globe, for five thousand years, the idea of human civilization without slavery was unimaginable . . . He saw the idea that all men and women are created equal by God, in his image, and are therefore sacred. He saw the idea that all men are brothers and that we are all our brothers' keepers. He saw the idea that one must love one's neighbor as oneself and that we must do unto others as we would have them do unto us . . . Wilberforce may perhaps be said to have performed the wedding ceremony between faith and culture that, in human reality, were nowhere in evidence.[8]

William Wilberforce is one of countless members of the church who stood against injustice in the culture around them. For every Martin Luther King Jr. or William Wilberforce there are countless Christians who stood courageously to change the world around them and left the culture hating the thing they once embraced. Today, our society stands for human rights but forgets that the root of human rights is found in faithful followers of Jesus throughout history. It is found in the simple idea that you are to love your neighbor as yourself.

FISH OUT OF WATER

Does a fish know it lives in water? It has lived in water its entire life. It was born into an ecosystem that utterly depends on water to live. Day in and day out it swims, breathes and exists in a sea of H_2O. It may swim to the surface occasionally but—in the end—it has no idea that water is the basis of its life. Living in water is all the fish has ever known, and water is so integrated into the fish's existence that it literally cannot see it.

This is the relationship our culture has to the "water" around it. To Jesus. To the church. Followers of Jesus have so affected the world around them that their impact is sometimes difficult to see.

We don't have to whitewash the areas the church has failed throughout history. And although the church shouldn't be about politics, that doesn't negate our responsibility to continue improving the world around us.

We need to remember there is an undeniable relationship between caring for the sick or abolishing slavery and the movement of Jesus. We need to take moments to see ourselves in the context of the amazing revolution of Jesus that affects kings and nations. This is what *he* does. This is what *we* do.

DAVID CROWDER

BORN AT CHURCH

Outside of my family, most of what I know of God and his activity here on planet Earth has been experienced within an organized community of believers. For the longest time, I held the strong belief that I was born in the nursery of First Baptist Church in Texarkana, Texas. I didn't hear the words, "Wadley Hospital on Stateline Avenue," until later, after it was already set in my little-boy mind that church is where family comes from.

Currently at this stage of life, with my educated adult-sized intelligence, I believe that's still a pretty great way to think about it. How are we to know God, the maker of the cosmos? How are we to see and believe that he is here and active? How are we to know and understand the meaning and intention of the words of Holy Scripture that we are hiding in our hearts? How do we have familiarity with the breath and movement of the Holy Spirit?

I think the biggest ideas of who God is and what he is up to in this wide world become real and tangible when they come to us in human form. He became touchable when my parents' church friends huddled with them, together, in the waiting room of Wadley Hospital, anticipating my arrival. He is there when those same friends gather graveside to bury their parents. He is there, and he is real, and he is weeping with us.

As I grew, I watched the people of that church, the one I was born into, be there, together, in all the best and worst of life—and there was intentionality to it. It was a community of people who loved one another and were trying to follow this person, Jesus, no matter what came their way.

In my pursuit of Jesus, the thing that has formed me most has been his people. The ones who are there with you in births and deaths and wins and losses and graduations and salvations and divorces and marriages and cancers and remissions. Real live people, with hearts beating and hands holding and songs flowing. The real, live, touchable activity of God. That is the local church for me.

[3]

HIS IDENTITY FOR US

Deep down we all hunger to know *who* we are. Not *what* we do or *how* others perceive us, but *who* we are. We continually try to talk about our identity through our work. "I am an architect" or "I am a pastor" or "I am a student." We may find our identity in our biological family. "I am a mom" or "I am an only child." But those titles always come up short. Sometimes we are great at our job. Sometimes we are not. We have moments of great parenting and moments of not-so-great parenting.

In our core, however, we know that these will never fulfill us. How we are doing in our job or our family is not *who* we are. What we or others around us think about us has no bearing on *who* we are.

There is a deep and profound difference between our identity and our actions. In Jesus, a divine exchange has left us with a new identity. And though this identity is brand new, it is actually ancient. Original. We get to go back before the fall of man. To the pure and unconditional love of God. We get to return to direct and undeserved connection to our creator.

> This is how God showed his love among us: He sent his one and only Son into the world that we might live through him. This is love: not that we loved God, but that he loved us and sent his Son as an atoning sacrifice for our sins. (1 John 4:9–10)

As followers of Jesus, we are called *sons and daughters of God* (2 Corinthians 6:18). We are *redeemed* and *forgiven* (Ephesians 1:7). We are *adopted* into a new kingdom (Ephesians 1:5; Colossians 1:13). We are loved by the God who created us, and nothing can separate us from him (Romans 8:38–39). That is *who* we are, regardless of our past, present, and future imperfections. Nothing can remove the identity we find *in* Christ.

NOT JUST YOU BUT US

One of the most important insights to have while reading the Bible is to remember that instruction is not always *just* for you personally but for the greater body as well. The Bible is not simply for the individual but also the corporate. Mark Dever, in his book *The Church: The Gospel Made Visible,* says it this way:

> More than once Jesus said that his people would demonstrate their love for him by obeying his commandments (Luke 24:46–48; Rev. 5:9). And the obedience which interests him is not only individual but corporate. Together individuals in churches will go, disciple, baptize, teach to obey, love, remember and commemorate his substitutionary death with the bread and the cup.

There are identities that God has for *us*. Not just an identity for *me* but for *we*. Things he says about the body of Christ that are irrevocable. Identities given to us individually as well as corporately.

So who does he say we are? Does he define us in the church by our flawed history? Our current imperfections? Or does he have a deeper identity for *his* church? For his people? Let's catch *his* vision for the church. Not a vision based on our *perception* but on the greater reality of the words that he speaks over us.

WE ARE LOVED

There is this profound parallel that Paul brings to the table in Ephesians 5. The love that Christ has for us—for his church—is like the love of a husband for his wife.

> No one abuses his own body, does he? No, he feeds and pampers it. That's how Christ treats us, the church, since we are part of his body. And this is why a man leaves father and mother and cherishes his wife. No longer two, they become "one flesh." This is a huge mystery, and I don't pretend to understand it all. What is clearest to me is the way Christ treats the church. And this provides a good picture of how each husband is to treat his wife, loving himself in loving her, and how each wife is to honor her husband. (Ephesians 5:29–33 MSG)

The deep and meaningful covenant of marriage, the bringing together of two individuals into one flesh, is a parallel for the love that Jesus has for his church. There is this beautiful mingling of two identities being intertwined into each other's lives. And Paul doesn't stop there.

Jesus loves and cares for us like he loves and cares for his own body.

The profound mystery is this: Jesus cares for his bride as he cares for himself. There is this great, divine mingling and blurriness between where God's love for Jesus starts and where his love for his church ends. His peace becomes our peace. His sacrifice becomes our sacrifice. His story becomes our story.

> With God on our side like this, how can we lose? If God didn't hesitate to put everything on the line for us, embracing our condition and exposing himself to the worst by sending his own Son, is there anything else he wouldn't gladly and freely do for us? And who would dare tangle with God by messing with one of God's chosen? Who would dare even to point a finger? The One who died for us—who was raised to life for us!—is in the presence of God at this very moment sticking up for us. (Romans 8:31–39 MSG)

Who would mess with us as God's children? His love runs as deep as blood. Like a father caring for his children.

Like a husband for his wife, he *loves* us. He protects us as a father fiercely protects his bullied child. This is the deep and profound love of God for us. For his church.

HE IS FAITHFUL

We have few things in life that are faithful. Reliable. All of our human relationships let us down at some point. Life circumstances change all around us. But there is one thing we can rely on. One place we can put down our anchor in stormy and uncertain seas.

> But Christ is faithful as the Son over God's house. And *we are his house*, if indeed we hold firmly to our confidence and the hope in which we glory. (Hebrews 3:6, emphasis added)

Jesus is *faithful*. Every day. Every hour. Year after year, he is faithful. And not just in our lives individually. He is faithful to his *church*. His house. He hasn't left us. He will never forsake us. No matter how unfaithful we may be, he remains faithful to us.

The prophet Hosea was called to live a life that echoed the faithfulness of God. In the first verse and chapter of the book of Hosea, God calls him to marry a prostitute. His ministry calling was to intertwine his life with a woman who was promiscuous. To a woman who was almost guaranteed to be unfaithful to him. This is to represent the relationship between God and Israel. God and his people. Hosea prophetically loved, pursued, and cared for his unfaithful wife just as God does with us. And through her unfaithfulness

Hosea proved his faithfulness. Through her marital wanderings she proved Hosea's relentless pursuit of her.

Jesus is *faithful*. Every day. Every hour. Year after year, he is faithful. And not just in our lives individually. He is faithful to his *church*.

And this is our relationship as bride to our groom. Church to Jesus. Through our unfaithfulness God proves his faithfulness. Through our wanderings we prove God's relentless pursuit of us. Is there anything that can separate us from the love of Christ?

HE LEADS

We have all seen leaders in the church who take on more than they should. To pastor a group of people is a difficult and weighty job, and it can lead to a lot of unhealthy ways to cope. Some leaders begin to get a big head and demand that everyone fall in line behind their lead. Some are so weighed down in their role that they burn out or have a nervous breakdown under the responsibility. Maybe most pastors experience a little of both.

For any church leader to stay sane, they must at some point confront (and continually revisit) the fact that *Jesus* "is the head of the body, the church" (Colossians 1:18). Jesus takes the weight of it on *his* shoulders. A weight that we were never meant to carry.

Pastoring a church is a heavy responsibility, but it is never the job of a leader to lead ahead of God. Leading outside of God's direction can produce pride, burnout, loss of relationships, and everything inbetween.

But all church leaders are human. Every leader is imperfect and will at some point wrestle with this. Understanding Jesus's leadership over the church is for the congregant just as much as it is for the leader. Expecting perfection from your pastor will end up harming you both.

THE DREADED COMMENT CARD

Having worked in a local church for a number of years now, there's not much I dread more than reading a "comment" card from people who seem to enjoy sharing a bit of criticism about the lights, volume, or sermon content.

Maybe the foyer is not inviting enough. Maybe the pastor talks too much about sports—or not enough about politics. Whatever the opinions, critics jot them down and throw them your way.

Not only that, but occasionally these folks feel free to judge your character while they're at it. Maybe your motivations in upgrading the sanctuary chairs are brought into question. Maybe they feel concerned about "pride" seeping into your heart. It's not only that they disagree with you, it's that they feel "concerned" about your motivations. The motivations that somehow give them special insight.

As a church leader there can be no lower feeling than to receive one of these. They can be one of the most difficult parts of a job you pour your heart into week after week. Sure, some of them are nice. And sometimes the criticism is valid and needs to be considered. But when you receive one, there is a strong temptation to bend to *all* of the critiques—to change the direction in which you sense God is leading, just to please the *people*.

Jesus is the head of the body. He is the leader who needs to be watched and listened to. A pastor who is following Jesus's lead will inevitably return time and time again to the words of the apostle Paul: "Am I now trying to win the approval of human beings, or of God? Or am

I trying to please people? If I were still trying to please people, I would not be a servant of Christ" (Galatians 1:10). A church leader who is looking to Jesus's lead and not the approval of man is a leader worth following. And a congregation that trusts the perfect leadership of Jesus becomes more graceful and loving toward its leader and, in turn, becomes a greater force for the gospel in its city.

The church stands redeemed and purchased. *You and I together* stand redeemed and purchased. Jesus died for *me*, but he also died for *us*.

So should we communicate with our pastor if we feel concerned? Of course. But we need to begin to emphasize relationship with one another over position or entitlement. Criticism should be brought face to face, allowing dialogue. Search out your own expectations and opinions and weigh how necessary it is to bring them up. As church leaders, we always appreciate a graceful and heart-felt concern. Especially over an anonymous message from the dreaded comment card!

JESUS DIED FOR THE CHURCH

We have all heard about Jesus's sacrifice for us individually. That he died on the cross to take our sins on himself. That he received the correction and punishment due to us so that we can walk in freedom. We have been saved from the death that sin produces so we can stand alive in his presence. Not because we earned it, but because of his great sacrifice to restore all things to himself. He loves *you* and gave himself up for *you*.

> Husbands, love your wives, just as Christ loved the church and gave himself up *for her* to make her holy, cleansing her by the washing with water through the word, and to present her to himself as a radiant church, without stain or wrinkle or any other blemish, but holy and blameless. (Ephesians 5:25–26, emphasis added)

This is the gospel that we have heard communicated a thousand different ways. In a thousand different settings. All of this is beautiful, and true. Scriptural. The gospel is for you and for me. But it's also for *us*.

The church stands redeemed and purchased. *You and I together* stand redeemed and purchased. Together, we are washed clean by his word. We will one day be presented to Jesus in the *perfection* we were created to have. One day *we* will be presented without spot or wrinkle because of Jesus's care for his bride. Jesus died for *me*, but he also died for *us*.

THE CHURCH IS POWERFUL

Most of us have read this passage of Scripture: "I will build my church, and the gates of Hades will not overcome it" (Matthew 16:18). We have heard sermons about how the powers of darkness can't prevail against us. But I wonder how many of us have truly looked at the phrasing of this passage. The "gates" of hell (or Hades) will not prevail. The *gates*. Gates are defensive, not offensive.

In light of polls and pop culture, the church has recently felt the need to go on the defensive. Many feel as though they need to fortify *our* gates. To keep *our* defenses high to protect *us* from attack. But the power of the gospel is meant to take the fight *to* the enemy. The power and love of Jesus is meant to break the four walls of the church—from the inside out—and take to the streets to see the gates of the enemy fail.

But what is "the fight"? What does "the battle" look like? Is it physical? Is it political? What if our power resides in the spirit of God, who dwells in us?

When Jesus said that the gates of hell won't prevail against us, he didn't say that there was something we should do to earn this power. He never laid out seven easy steps to a powerful church or created a prospectus on the powerful potential of the church you *could* join. He said that we *are* powerful. He said that *he* would build it, and because of that we are powerful. It is an amazing inheritance we can walk in all the time. It's part of our identity. It's who we are as the body of Christ.

When we rely on Jesus and put our trust in him, we receive all that we need: "Praise be to the God and Father of our Lord Jesus Christ, who has blessed us in the heavenly realms with every spiritual blessing in Christ" (Ephesians 1:3). We are already equipped with all we need to be powerful. In our day-to-day. In our work. In our family. In our church. *Power.* It is already a part of your identity whether you believe it or not. Whether you walk in it or not.

The beauty of this power is that it is diverse, and God multiplies its strength when each of us comes together as one body. Everyone playing their part. Everyone part of the whole but wonderfully unique. Everyone with a little power on their own . . . but when that power is combined, an unstoppable force is created. A weight that the gates of the enemy cannot hold back.

They say a snowflake weighs approximately 0.001–0.003 grams. By itself, it has little to it. Small in size. Light in weight. It's difficult to even see an individual snowflake when it's snowing. A single one is beautiful and unique but doesn't make much of an impact. But when billions of snowflakes come together, they become weighty. Snow can crush the roof of a house or even an industrial building. In fact, snow causes billions of dollars of damage in the United States annually. One small, one-of-a-kind flake becomes an unstoppable force.

This is the power of the church. This is the power of *our* family. The movement that we are a part of. This is who we are whether we *feel* it or not. If we lose ground politically we are still powerful. If we lose congregants and slip in the cultural polls, it doesn't change the *identity* of the church. She is still the bride. Flawed but beautiful. Imperfect but powerful. We have amazing days of power ahead of us. Not because we've earned it. Not because we are more relevant or accepted. But because *that* is the identity given to us *from* Jesus, and nothing can separate us from it.

JENN JOHNSON
BETHEL MUSIC

COMMUNITY IS KINGDOM

There's not really one story of how community has impacted my life, but I know community has gotten me to where I am today. My story is still being written, and it's a beautiful picture of the kingdom.

Community is kingdom. We all have different gifts, and we need each other. Romans 12:4–5 reminds us, "For just as each of us has one body with many members, and these members do not all have the same function, so in Christ we, though many, form one body, and each member belongs to all the others." When we have a community of people walking in their gifts, we see the body of Christ functioning. God has given us each gifts to hone, and it's part of our calling as followers of Christ to recognize the gifts of those around us and to champion them in each other. He wants us to realize we need each other and that we need to help others strengthen their gifts.

Since we are made in the image of God—and we are made like Him—there is greatness in all of our lives. Instead of being intimidated by others' greatness, we celebrate the greatness within our lives and the lives of those around us. We defeat jealousy and unhealthy comparison when we choose to strengthen and encourage one other. Galatians 5:26 speaks measures on living a yielded life in the Holy Spirit:

> Since this is the kind of life we have chosen, the life of the Spirit, let us make sure that we do not just hold it as an idea in our heads or a sentiment in our hearts, but work out its implications in every detail of our lives. That means we will not compare ourselves with each other as if one of us were better and another worse. We have far more interesting things to do with our lives. Each of us is an original. (MSG)

I've seen transformation and support in my community through the strength of His people. I'm so thankful for the longevity in my current relationships, which include life-long friendships from a very young age. Navigating and keeping many intimate relationships in your life isn't the easiest, but the fruit of being surrounded by community is worth it all. In my life's journey, I've had tough seasons. I'm thankful for the people who've been there for me to just love me, give an encouraging word, correct me, or pray for me. I would have been in such a dark hour had it not been for those people surrounding and supporting me.

I think that community is an expression of God's heart. God loves it when we spend time alone with him, drawing near, listening to his heart, and sitting in his presence. In the same way, community also brings him great joy because through it he is revealed in new ways throughout the body of Christ.

[4]

SHE IS NOT PERFECT

If you are an artist, you go to other artists' work for inspiration. You may scan through many different works of art until you find the one that sticks out to you. The one that makes you say, "Whoa, that's great!" Maybe you start copying it in your art. *Blatantly*. Soon you begin to incorporate that artist's style into your own work. Then you see something else you like. All of a sudden you are off and going in a new direction and . . . *boom* it's yours. Your art becomes something gloriously unique that reflects *you*. Something that began as an obvious rip-off is now something one of a kind.

Maybe you preach and you get inspiration from another sermon. Maybe you write music and you begin with inspiration from another musician you love and admire. This is all part of the creative process. Using others for inspiration is what sets great artists apart from good ones. Pablo Picasso once said, "Bad artists copy. Good artists steal."

We do this all the time in church. With podcasts, blogs, books, and music streaming you can get all of the inspiration you want. There are churches that excel in getting new people plugged in. There are churches that are creative and ground-breaking in the areas of media or worship music. There are churches known for reaching the lost and preaching the gospel. No matter what you need inspiration for, you can find it.

You don't have to be a pastor to seek out this sort of creative input. Even church attendees and volunteers look for this same inspiration for their own community. They listen to other preachers, go to conferences, and read books to grow in their walk with God and learn principles to share with church leaders or friends.

And all of that is healthy. It's not only healthy, but it shows that you want to grow in the art of leading a church well. Or *attending* a church well. Being a force for the gospel in your city and doing it with excellence.

But can you take it too far? At what point does inspiration end and unrealistic expectations begin?

"I HEARD THIS GREAT PODCAST . . ."

I spend a lot of time in local church leadership meetings. A *lot* of time. I have sat under and alongside many pastors. At some point in a meeting, after we have all thoroughly vented our frustrations or talked about all of the areas we could have improved that weekend, someone asks, "Has anyone listened to the latest message from _____?" or says, "I heard this great podcast on _____."

And as the years go by there emerges a list of the usual suspects. *Oh, there goes Bob again talking about* _____. Or *There goes Sue, again, about* _____. Just fill in the blank. They obviously admire certain churches or pastors or worship leaders. But why wouldn't they? We have large, amazing churches to look up to all around us. Churches that influence culture and have a calling on them that inspires us to do greater and push harder.

But it can cross into territory that isn't healthy. I often hear people—and am guilty of this myself on occasion—compare their pastors to a pastor they've heard on a podcast or one whose book they have read. There comes a moment when they build a "perfect" leader in their head that isn't based on reality. They begin to imagine that this leadership guru or that best-selling author does all the right things, and they project this perceived perfection onto their own pastors.

At some point, pastors begin to feel these unrealistic expectations mount up: *You need to preach better. Lead better. Be more gracious. Confront people more. Talk more about the Holy Spirit. Focus more on this issue or that one.* You name it.

This creates a pressure and insecurity that doesn't just land on them. As they take on these expectations, they begin to create their own in turn. They build expectations around perfect staff or congregations. *Do we need to hire better people? Maybe we need new elders. I just need a better worship team. I wish I had a more worshipful or mature congregation.* And on and on. These unrealistic expectations begin to seep into every pore of their church and are soon felt by the whole community.

Subconsciously we begin to feel restless, as if we are missing out on being a part of a *better* church somewhere else. Anywhere but where we've landed. We begin to replace the *actual* people in our lives with mannequins of "perfection." This isn't reality, and it keeps us from truly diving into our community. So we continue to hold everyone at arm's length.

Over the years I've had the privilege of working with not only leaders of small churches but of large, international ones as well. They were and are filled with amazing and gifted people. But all of them—without fail—come up short somewhere. Every church leader—including the ones we look up to and admire—is *imperfect*. There are strengths and weaknesses in every person, and you find them out the closer you are to them.

EXPECTATIONS KILL RELATIONSHIPS

My wife took some parenting classes at a local church when our first son was born. We were new parents and were hungry for any parental wisdom we could get ahold of! She would come home each time and tell me some of the things she learned. It was all great stuff, but honestly I have forgotten most of the teaching. Except for this one phrase: *expectations kill relationships*. And I'd sharpen the pencil a bit to say, *unrealistic* expectations kill relationships. The principle is this: if you go into a store with your two-year-old and *expect* that he won't see a toy he wants and throw a massive tantrum in the middle of the store when the aforementioned toy is not purchased, you may find yourself in trouble! You will have no plan to deal with the situation because your unrealistic expectation caused you to not have a strategy on dealing with it beforehand! It's a two-year-old! Tantrums are their specialty. Expect it! Plan for it!

It is the same in the local church. When we walk into relationships with unhealthy expectations only to see those expectations dashed, we act surprised. Worse, we often simply dump those relationships and try to find others to measure up. No church is as perfect as you imagine it is. *No* church. When you expect that from the beginning, then you are able to plan for how to deal with it before things go wrong. In turn, having realistic expectations creates more commitment to your community.

Unrealistic expectations lead to churches where people aren't committed and leaders are constantly worn out and insecure. They also create a monochromatic church experience around the country, where congregations loosely copy one another to avoid taking risks in finding their own voices in the midst of their communities. Finding inspiration to push you toward excellence is wonderful. Pursuing a perceived perfection at the cost of finding what makes your church unique is not. The power of the local church is in its diversity. It's in the beauty and messiness of it all where we find true connection and commitment to one another.

COUNT THE COST

Is there anyone here who, planning to build a new house, doesn't first sit down and figure the cost so you'll know if you can complete it? If you only get the foundation laid and then run out of money, you're going to look pretty foolish. Everyone passing by will poke fun at you. (Luke 14:28–30 MSG)

Counting the cost with Jesus is not just about following him, but about joining his body. Committing to working with the imperfect carriers of a perfect grace. This commitment must be counted before you can build. But you have to know at the start that it is worth it. The heart and maturity forged in a person who commits to a community, through the good and the bad, is something that is unsurpassed. Those who stick it out find a treasure on the other side they didn't expect. God created an imperfect church for a reason. The trials of commitment refine you and create strength and wisdom.

> Unrealistic expectations lead to churches where people aren't committed and leaders are constantly worn out and insecure.

At OUTCRY, we connect with a lot of church leaders all over the country. From all kinds of generational and denominational backgrounds. All of them carry their own imperfections and past baggage. But across the board, they come to the table with a heart for Jesus and their church. Each night of our tour, we see the body of Christ come together. City after city, people join one another to worship Jesus. And despite individual imperfections, they collectively make a beautiful sound.

We need to view the local church not only as individual but as a significant part of the universal beauty of the church. What I love so much about OUTCRY is that each night I get to see imperfect churches around the world join together to make a beautiful sound for God—as one. Getting vision for this begins with us grasping the significance of *our* church. When we commit to *our* church we commit to *the* church.

AT LEAST WE AREN'T LIKE *THAT* CHURCH

When people don't engage in relationships, they tend to judge others' hearts, motives, and actions. The further the distance the better. Not only this, but the greater the platform their "targets" have, the easier it is to hit them with their arrows of criticism.

Maybe you've experienced this yourself and have been on the receiving end of the attacks. If you or your church carry great influence, you'll discover a great number of people there to give you their "opinion." The *should haves* and *could haves* come your way in greater and greater numbers as you have greater impact.

Or maybe you've gone on the offensive yourself at

one point or another (I know I have been guilty of this). Whether it is the church down the street or an internationally known ministry, we sometimes feel great freedom to "knock them down a peg" by sharing all the things they do wrong or not well enough. This is the other side of the same coin we discussed in the last section. But instead of comparing ourselves to the perceived *perfect* church, we compare ourselves to a perceived *defective* church.

The church is full of great influencers today. When it comes to social media and mass communication, there are churches gifted in those areas that utilize them to communicate the message of Jesus in new and fresh ways. In creative ways that not only fill their churches with people but also begin to fill stadiums. They begin to sell out tours. And as influence grows, so does the watchful eye of those in the church eagerly looking for something to critique.

But megachurches aren't the only ones under scrutiny. There are also small and average-sized churches down the street doing things differently. They, too, may have unique leaders and approaches to sharing the message of Jesus. Sometimes we notice bodies of believers growing rapidly. Or maybe they are shrinking in numbers. We are tempted to envy one church or diagnose issues in another. Our attention shifts from what God is doing in our church and community to what he is or isn't doing in another. We engage in a sort of divine gossip that ultimately makes us feel superior in some way.

I believe we are entering a season where the people of God are turning from this attitude. One of the most amazing things about OUTCRY is the fact that these major leaders from all over the world gather in one place. They worship together in a small group before the night begins, then hit the stage in unity. They put aside theological and cultural differences (which they *do* have) and stand supporting and loving one another.

There is an irrevocable identity that the universal church carries. That each *local* church carries. Whether big or small. Whether growing or shrinking. Every church is still part of the family. It is still a part of *his* body and *his* bride.

MOTIVE

I have heard many leaders—sometimes myself—talk about large churches and the people who run them. Not just whether or not they like those megachurch pastors and leaders. Not simply surface critique, but a discussion about their hearts and motives. Worship leaders and speakers are especially notorious about this. The discussion may simply begin with how other leaders dress but then becomes a seemingly spiritual exposition from there. We may discuss how much of a "show" other leaders put on. Or their "rock star" worship leader mentality. We just want to know "where their heart is" or that their "heart is for the Lord" first and foremost.

In 2007 I began working with nationally known worship leaders, doing art and Web design for them. I remember being amazed at how down to earth they were. Sure, there were imperfections and moments of humanity, but I remember actually being surprised at their humanness. Then, as the years went by, I began hanging out with more and more national influencers in the church. Shane introduced me to more worship leaders, and I began to see a pattern. As I witnessed the amazing, approachable nature of groups like Jesus Culture or heard Hillsong preach the gospel every night, I began to see an amazing behind-the-scenes nature of these leaders that blew me away.

Something shifted in me. After that, when I would hear a leader dive into the "holy" evaluation or motive analysis of other leaders, I would suddenly jump to their defense. Critique outside of relationship began rubbing me the wrong way. There is always another side to the story, and sometimes the behind-the-scenes is more pure and approachable than we imagine.

This feeling has only grown within me since we started OUTCRY. I've now met and worked with so many leaders who blow me away. And not just because of their ability to perform or preach—I have experienced firsthand their incredible heart for Jesus and his church. Judgment outside of relationships is easy, but the closer you are to people the harder it is to cast judgment on them. The closer you are to them, the more you see the nuances and heart behind their lives and actions.

THE POWER OF COMMITMENT

You may have reached this point in the book and are asking, "Ryan, are you saying we can't critique *anything*?" Not at all. "Doesn't God issue warnings to his people?" Of course he does. "Don't we have to go through seasons of change?" Yes, change is necessary at times, even coming on the back of critique. But the *way* you carry out criticism is as important as delivering it. Critique only carries power when given inside of the context of commitment and relationship.

Let's put it this way: Imagine I choose to talk to my wife about something I see in her life that isn't good, something I think she needs to change. Now, it isn't something that's catastrophic to our relationship, but it is a detail of her life I take seriously and something I know that is important to her as well. Now, if I say, "Blake, I see this problem in your life, which I think you need to change. I love you, and I am committed to helping you along the way because I just want to see you whole and well." This is a critique delivery worth listening to. There is a heart of commitment and love coming from me, giving my critique power.

This never happens, but . . . What if I have been on the road with OUTCRY for a month and haven't even had time for any serious conversations with my wife? Then when I get home, she hugs and kisses me and asks, "How are you? I've missed you! How was the tour?" Then suddenly I remember this thing that I don't like that she does. Again, it isn't catastrophic to the relationship— it's just something I prefer, but it is decently important to me. So I respond, "I've been meaning to talk to you about this. I see this problem in your life, and I think you need to change it. Now I love you, but I've been considering other relationships—you know, to keep my options open—and if you don't change this thing, I will probably leave you. Are we still cool?" This is *not* a critique worth listening to. It is not based in love or commitment, so it carries no power. It may be a good suggestion, but it is overshadowed by the bigger issue: lack of commitment.

WHAT DOES IT MATTER?

But what about the leaders we do know personally? What if we have a relationship with local leaders and *suspect greatly* that their motives are skewed? Maybe they seem to not be in it for Jesus but for themselves. They hint at money, fame, or influence a little too much. We've seen *that* side of them, and it isn't pretty.

Years back, God spoke something simple but profound to me. It was in a section of Scripture I'd read a hundred times. But this day I happened to be wrestling with what to say or not say to another leader. God usurped my logic and spoke something that seemed almost un-Christian. Something very contrary to the church culture I was in. In Philippians 1:15–18, Paul says:

It is true that some preach Christ out of envy and rivalry, but others out of goodwill. The latter do so out of love, knowing that I am put here for the defense of the gospel. The former preach Christ out of selfish ambition, not sincerely, supposing that they can stir up trouble for me while I am in chains. But what does it matter? The important thing is that in every way, whether from false motives or true, Christ is preached. And because of this I rejoice.

With God there is always a *third* way. He seems to take our logic that could go into two different camps and offers another way. And it isn't always a compromise between the two. It's not always the path in between the others. It seems to come from above. A way almost hidden, but once you find it, it becomes self-evident. You see it all around you.

This scripture is a *third* way. The motive of other people is something we could never *truly* know. In fact, sometimes we aren't even aware of our own motives. Proverbs 21:2 says, "Every way of a man is right in his own eyes, *but the Lord weighs the heart*" (emphasis mine). He is the only one who can weigh the heart. Our job is not to look from afar—or even up close—and analyze the motives of people. We need to rejoice in the fact that people—even imperfectly motivated people like us—are talking about Jesus.

And yes, Scripture talks about confronting *sin* in someone's life. There are times when this is necessary in a community. But motive is something different. Something hidden to everyone but God. We need to "wonder what's going on in their heart" less and seek God about our own motives more. We need to worry less about what's hidden in another and concern ourselves with how to serve each other more.

Motive is something we can't know or control in other people. And Jesus knew we would have a propensity to get bogged down in the things we can't control. He knew that we would gravitate toward solving the problems of others. He offers us another way. A way of less burden and worry: "Therefore do not worry about tomorrow, for tomorrow will worry about itself. Each day has enough trouble of its own" (Matthew 6:34).

Today has enough worries for itself. *Your* community has enough issues to work through. *Your* motives and desires need prayer and attention today. We all have a job in front of us. Our local church. Our small group. Our upcoming missions trip. Whatever it may be. Being the judge of others and their motives only slows us down. Distracts us from the impact we could be making today.

PLAN TO STAY

In OUTCRY our desire is to see an uprising of local churches influencing their neighborhood and city. Not being bogged down by the unrealistic expectations of our church or its leaders. Not being distracted by the never-satisfied critique of others. We see an imperfect but beautiful church filled with diverse expressions of Jesus on every street. There is beauty in the imperfect. Beyond that, there is beauty in *committing yourself* to the imperfect.

On a church-to-church level, we see pastors and congregations committing to love and champion one another. To lift them up without feeling the temptation to critique outside of relationship. On a local level, we see people committing to their church and community despite the imperfections they have.

Any community around us will have imperfect leaders and imperfect congregations, but giving our church or community around us only half of our heart sells us and them short. We miss opportunity. When we commit to our church—truly *dive in*—something powerful happens. We begin to make a real impact. A meaningful impact on friends, family, and community. And as we put in years of commitment to a community of imperfect people (including our imperfect selves), something will be forged in us that couldn't be forged otherwise.

> There is beauty in the imperfect. Beyond that, there is beauty in *committing yourself* to the imperfect.

Are there legitimate reasons to leave a church? Yes. And that is something between you and the Holy Spirit. There are reasons to knock the dust off of your shoes and move on. I am not advocating the condemnation of yourself or others who go through the difficult season of leaving a church.

However, if you find yourself *planning* on leaving when you get there, or holding the community at arm's length in anticipation of a future church hop, pause and pray. Pray that God will open your eyes to see your church, not as you see it, but as *he* sees it. God may be speaking to you now about your expectations. About the importance of commitment. Allow for the possibility that God may be bringing you to a season of committing deeper to your church community. To finding beauty *through* imperfections, not despite them.

Maybe you need to start *planning* on staying. The local church is worth it. It is a worthy and significant calling to give your whole life to. And I believe that as more and more of us commit to what's in front of us—to the local church God is calling us to—we will see a new chapter and movement of God unlike anything we have seen yet. The next big thing is here. It's always been here. It's *you*. It's *us*. It's *Him*. Let's dive in.

CHRIS QUILALA
JESUS CULTURE

WALKING BY OUR SIDE

In September 2014 we started a church called Jesus Culture in Sacramento with the blessing of our home church—Bethel in Redding, California. My wife, Alyssa, and I were there from the beginning with a group of people navigating how to build a church from nothing. At the time, Alyssa and I had two beautiful little girls, and in July of that year we found out that we had a little boy on the way. We were overjoyed and felt as though our son would complete our family.

Right after Thanksgiving, when Alyssa was almost eight months pregnant, we went up to Redding to see our friends, where we have an annual dinner we like to call "friendsgiving." It was a busy day of cooking and an evening full of laughs and good food. As the night settled down, my wife was waddling through the house when she looked at me with great concern and said, "I don't think I've felt Jethro [our son] kick or move today." So we began to talk to him, sing to him, poke her belly, most of the things that normally got big kicks from him! After a while of not feeling anything, we decided we needed to head to the ER. We were sure everything was fine, but we needed to gain peace of mind.

As soon as we got to the ER, they strapped her to a fetal heartbeat monitor. There was no heartbeat. The nurse explained that sometimes the baby is hiding, but an ultrasound would help them see what was going on. When the doctor came in and started the ultrasound, we saw our son's perfect nose, fully formed body, and even could see his curly hair. The doctor was quiet. The room was quiet. Then we heard the worst sentence we've ever heard: "Your son has no heartbeat; he's gone." After a completely normal pregnancy, with no complications, our boy was dead for no explainable reason. We had just heard his heart beating less than a week prior. We were completely shocked.

In that moment we felt a pain we had never experienced. A grief that overtook us to the point of complete devastation. But right away we said, "No. We're going to believe that God is going to do something. We are going to believe that God will do a miracle."

So we called our church family in Sacramento and

told our friends and community in Redding. And everyone rushed to be at our side. We worshipped and prayed vehemently for a miracle. We were imploring heaven for the miraculous intervention of Jesus. And in the midst of it we bounced between great hope and the heavy weight of the situation.

After two days of inducing labor, we went through the final push, holding on to the hope that he would take a breath of life when he came into the world. Our son, Jethro Dylan Quilala, was stillborn.

Even after the delivery we had our pastors and community around us praying and worshipping with us. And in that moment—as a worshipper—I chose to still believe in the God who is able to perform miracles. At his memorial we sang "10,000 Reasons (Bless the Lord)" as a command over our hearts and the situation. It's easy to sing "mountain high valley low" when you're on the mountain, but the test of the heart is singing those words when we're in the valley.

But in the wake of this tragic moment in our lives, our church community came immediately to our side. Our brand-new church—not even six months old—began bringing us meals, calling, visiting, and praying for us. They truly rallied to our side. And we found ourselves saying, "I can't imagine going through this alone." First we had God's presence comforting us, but second we had the support of our church family surrounding us when we needed it most.

In April 2015 I had a dream. I dreamt that I approached a songwriter whom I had just met and asked him, "What song are we writing?" and he replied, "Oh, this song is 'Miracles.'" So the next day we began to work on the song that we called "Miracles."

I am convinced that God does not change even when our situations do. During that season, we didn't get stuck on asking why. For me to sing, "I believe in you, I believe in you, you're the God of miracles" even when I didn't see the miracle, was something I *needed* to proclaim because deep down I still believed it.

But it wasn't just a message that I needed to process. Our church was walking, believing, and praying passionately for us. So when the miracle didn't happen, that proclamation of still believing in the God of the miraculous needed to be sung by *them* too. What God did in our lives during that season spilled out on the church family around us so that we could all stand together and sing "You're the God of miracles."

[5]

IT WILL GET MESSY

Now, OUTCRY itself initially started years ago with Shane Quick. It was a Bible study that eventually turned into an event that brought different churches together. It came from humble beginnings and spread through grassroots efforts. But as quick—pun intended—as it began, God spoke to Shane that OUTCRY was to be shut down and resurrected later in a different form.

That's when I came in. *OUTCRY 2.0: The Resurrection* (as the movie title would say).

In January 2015, after years of us praying and not being certain about whether OUTCRY would in fact see life again, God clearly laid out a path before us. And though it had not been a tour up until that point, it became quite clear that God wanted us to take our message *to* the people. From city to city—twelve to be exact. Once the vision was shared, the first artists we heard from who wanted to join us were Hillsong United, Kari Jobe, and Jesus Culture. Just these three would have been an amazing start. A lineup that surpassed our expectations. But as the days and weeks went by we heard yeses from Crowder, Bethel, Passion, Lauren Daigle, and Trip Lee. Once God said *yes*, it was like we couldn't stop it.

But along with all of this excitement and momentum came the immense task of *starting*. By the end of February the tour was in full planning mode, and as the plan unfolded we saw that the optimum time for the tour was just five months away. *Five months* to take the largest worship tour in history off the ground. The task was immense and at times quite messy.

Yes, God was clearly in it. Yes, we had an amazing team of professionals—in fact, some of the best in the world—working with us. But in the end there were very few of us who *carried* the vision at that time. Few to infect the many on the team with our heart for the church. This meant that the team needed lots of one-on-one time with those of us who founded the tour.

As we finished promo videos and social media campaigns and the day of the tour kickoff drew near, it became overwhelming. The list of to-do items seemed never-ending, and by the time we hit the road many of us were already exhausted. And it rolled over to our first show in Chicago.

The venue in the Windy City was outdoors and had a curfew. A curfew that had *no* grace. If we went one minute over, they would simply shut down our power. As our first night progressed we continued to run later and later with the curfew looming ever closer! There were lots of spur-of-the-moment changes and tempers flaring as we ran around backstage trying desperately to keep it all together. The night progressed to Hillsong United hitting the stage. As they finished, a man from the venue took station at our proverbial power switch and stared at his watch, waiting for the clock to hit 11:01 so he could shut off our power. The pressure kept mounting until Hillsong hit their final chord at 11:00 and 30 seconds! We had made it by the skin of our teeth. But we returned to our tour bus dejected and tired. What a way to kick off. I had an overwhelming urge to go crawl into a hole somewhere.

But as the days progressed, we got our sea legs and began to finish our nights on time. We started to see less mess and more beauty. Attempting a tour that had never been attempted before and bringing together some of the most influential church leaders on one stage was no easy task. We were imperfect humans trying to keep it together in the midst of an immense call. But I knew deep down that it was God's calling for us. We could clearly see God's hand in the timing, the speed of it coming together, and the heart that was coming through night after night. To my surprise, though, it didn't *feel* good many nights.

This kind of messiness is unavoidable in the kingdom. Especially when we step out of the boat and pursue Jesus in the stormy waters.

Most of the time when God calls us to *start* something, we walk into it not fully knowing what lies ahead. We may be experienced or have a great team, but ultimately when God calls us to what our friends at Hillsong call *the great unknown*, we are always confronted with our own inability to accomplish that calling alone. Our inability *without him* becomes a glaring—and healthy—reminder of our shortcomings.

Often in the local church, we imagine that the "big" churches (or worship leaders or speakers) don't deal with mess. We think that bigger budgets and greater talents mean that everything sails along without a hitch. But this isn't true. The nature of the local church is messy no matter what the size. When we give our life to the church—to Jesus—we will inevitably have confrontations.

We will see people slip into sin and find ourselves

diving into *their* mess. Or slip into sin ourselves and need to invite others into *our* mess. But Jesus never told us that ministry would be clean and tidy. In fact, the people he chose to lead created huge messes.

BUILT ON A MESS

Jesus didn't exactly choose the cream of the crop for his disciples. He put together a team that most church leaders would find iffy at best. A group of guys messing up left and right. Fighting and trying to one-up each other. A motley crew of *real* guys with *real* problems.

You've got "sons of thunder" James and John—with help from their mom—trying to sell out the other disciples to be the most important two guys in Jesus's kingdom (Matthew 20:20–23). This didn't exactly cause them to be the most popular with the other disciples. Matthew had one of the most despised professions of that time. He was a tax collector (Matthew 10:3), and in Roman times tax collectors were often known to collect more taxes than they needed so that they could line their pockets with the extra money they collected. And then there was Peter. He was prone to outbursts (John

> Most of the time when God calls us to *start* something, we walk into it not fully knowing what lies ahead.

18:10), he vehemently denied being a follower of Jesus (Luke 22:54–62), and he provoked Jesus to call him *Satan* (Matthew 16:23). Overall, they weren't exactly the most reliable or mature group of guys.

In Matthew 26 when Jesus is first arrested, he gives a speech about how powerful his Father in heaven is. That at Jesus's command angels could descend and free him. But he chose to be in the position he was in to fulfill scriptures. And after this confident message about the power of God and the prophetic events about to take place, the Bible says, "Then all the disciples deserted him and fled." They ran and hid. When the going got tough the disciples got going.

These guys were a mess. They had a *long* way to go.

And yet, Jesus doesn't wait for the mess to get better. He doesn't wait for the disciples to be "ready" for the immense task he has for them. He actually *leaves* them after only a few years of working with them. He leaves them to begin his movement. His trust in the Holy Spirit is so great that he takes this group of disciples—falling apart at the seams—and leaves them to tell everyone on earth about him. He has to know it is going to get messy. He has to know they will make mistake after mistake as they go. But Jesus—the one who should be the most sensitive and cautious about the start of the movement he cares so much for—inexplicably allows the mess. This is the *foundation* of his church. Jesus seems to be unconcerned with the clearly-not-ready leaders leading the way in spreading his gospel to the nations. The church itself was *built* on eleven (twelve minus Judas) amazingly messy leaders.

If Jesus is at peace with the mess, why aren't we? What is it that compels us to try to clean up everything? What causes us to expect that there won't be difficult situations in the local church? It seems as though we expect there to be no arguments with unclear answers. Or leaders who show an ugly side. Or complaints about the volume of worship (I know, sensitive subject). These are the things that make church life difficult and often bring up real questions with no real answers. This is the messiness of church life that can make you feel like giving up and hanging out at a coffee shop on Sundays.

But if we are to be true disciples of Jesus, we need to expect and eventually *thrive* in the mess.

PRESENT HER TO HIMSELF

Daniel, one of the elders at my church, is one of those guys who loves and thrives in the world of theology. Anytime we hang out or talk, he takes my neat and clean theological conclusion and adds, "Yes, but have you read this book? Or this verse?" Voices such as his have added depth to my knowledge of Scripture and allowed me to see the "other side" with grace and understanding.

One day we were talking about the scripture where Paul speaks of "the spotless bride." As our conversation continued he pointed out a few key words in Ephesians, which started me on a path to a new understanding of the church. Many times we talk about Jesus returning for a spotless bride. Coming back for a church that has worked hard to perfect herself. But notice the language in Ephesians:

> Husbands, love your wives, just as Christ loved the church and gave himself up for her to make her holy, *cleansing her* by the washing with water through the word, and to present her *to himself* as a radiant church, without stain or wrinkle or any other blemish, but holy and blameless. (Ephesians 5:25–27, emphasis added)

Notice that it is *he* who is doing the cleansing. It's *he* who is presenting a spotless bride *to himself.* There is no promise in Scripture that we can find the perfect church. There is no promise that perfection will be attained in this age of the church. But as we commit to one another in the local church, and as we pursue Christ *together,* we will begin to find more beauty than we saw before. We will begin to see one another with more grace, even through times seasoned by confrontation and difficulty with people different than ourselves.

Is it easy? No. Will it get messy and unclear at times? Yes. But it is worth it. I haven't always approached it perfectly, and I have messed up in church community more times than I can count. But the years of me sticking it out in the local church—despite arguments, difficult situations, and differing opinions—have forged something in me I would never have seen otherwise.

This is insight that I received because of my grounding in my local church. God has used the church like this often in my life. A lunch with an elder, leader, or congregation member that ends with a new revelation from God. The local church keeps me grounded. It keeps *you* grounded. It will continue to challenge and grow you, if you continue to dive deeper and commit more of yourself to it.

THE LIGHTHOUSE

There is something innate in church life that opens you up to the ugly side of humanity. The outcasts and downtrodden—the people at the end of themselves looking for *someone* who can help them—often end up at the door of a church. They know little about God but are over-whelmed by the mess in their lives. All they can see are the areas they know they have irreparably messed up, and they see no way out. For many of them, despite how they were raised, the church represents help when they don't know where to turn.

This is why a church building on the corner with a steeple still has an important role in the kingdom. For the people on the edge and in need of an encounter with God, it's a clear destination. It's the beacon for the lost. The lighthouse on a rocky landing.

We've found it easy lately to disparage churches that spend money on a building. Wouldn't that money be better spent on the poor? Or missions? Or evangelism? That may be true for your church. It may genuinely be how God is leading your community and how he wants you to represent the heartbeat of your people. If so, more power to you! But before you cast judgment on the church next door that does have a building, remember that we serve a God of unlimited resources. Can he not afford a *physical* representation of his movement in every neighborhood on earth?

One of the beautiful things about a church building is that it *attracts* the messy and hopeless. They know where to go when they feel lost. And this can keep us grounded as we consistently connect with people who need it. I have seen this happen time and again at my church.

BACK TO THE MESS

After I got back from OUTCRY in 2015, I was reeling. We had an incredible trip around the country in front of crowds of ten thousand night after night with a lot of my heroes in the worship world. I was tired but also recharged and excited to see what God was doing on a large scale around the country. It felt huge, and I was excited to tell everyone I could about it.

The next day, I was back in my church office and chomping at the bit to tell anyone about what I just experienced. Then my phone rang. It was our receptionist, Anna, with a "pastor on call."

> One of the beautiful things about a church building is that it *attracts* the messy and hopeless. They know where to go when they feel lost.

Have you ever had God completely crash in on whatever mood you are in and bring something out of left field? That's what happened to me that morning. At our church "pastor on call" means that there is someone who has walked off the street and needs to talk with someone. And I was that someone.

Now, these have classically not gone well for me. I've

had people follow me around the campus yelling and cursing at me or had awkward conversations with drug addicts looking for money, not help. Many times I finish a messy meeting and pray for them and try my best to minister to them, but no matter how hard I try, these walk-ins don't often end well. So needless to say, I was not looking forward to it.

As I walked into our front office, I was greeted by a young woman who had just found out that she was unexpectedly expecting. She had been living with her mom but had now been kicked out. She then had moved on to her dad's place but was told she could only be there temporarily. She looked *tired,* and there were no clean answers to her questions. And having been on a tour bus the previous two weeks wasn't helping me find answers. But I dug deep and prayed with her and reminded her that God was not done with her. That she could have something that she thought was completely out of her grasp—*hope.* I connected her with a ministry at our church that helps young, single moms, which is infinitely more equipped than I to handle such a situation. Then I said goodbye and told her I'd be praying for her.

It wasn't much. It took all of twenty minutes. But as I walked out of the office I felt such a sense of peace. And not a self-aggrandizing sort of feeling. Not that I had

reached *down* to her from my high horse of moral supe-
riority, but I reached *out* to her as a follower of Jesus who
had received the grace, hope, and peace she needed. And
in that moment God gave me a peace and grounding that
I needed after the maiden voyage of OUTCRY. It was as if
God was reminding me, "Ryan, I was in OUTCRY and all
of its *bigness*. But remember the bigness of what I'm doing through all of the churches around the world that are
diligent in the *small*."

The mystery of the church is that it's *huge* but built
on the foundation of the *small*. The consistent, everyday
ministry. The church is ministering to people one-on-one
constantly around the world. Twenty-four hours a day,
seven days a week with love, hope, and redemption. As
you are reading this, there are followers of Jesus ministering to people with love, compassion, and power. In your
city. Across the country. All around the world. Right now.

This is the local church at work. Getting into messes
of real people in real need. We don't have to have all of the
answers—we just need to be available. We need to be
willing to not only get into the mess of the lost who walk
through our doors, but to get into one another's lives.
From follower of Jesus to follower of Jesus. Not being surprised when one of us steps in it. Not holding each other
accountable from our high horses, but getting down on

one another's level and bearing one another's burdens.

As David Stockton, the pastor at my church, puts it, standing shoulder to shoulder we need to get *under* one another's burdens. Not to stand on the outside and *tell* them how to lift better, but to actually get down with them and *carry* some of their weight. This way is difficult and it gets messy.

Take this idea a bit further, though. What about church to church and pastor to pastor? Leaders of churches reaching out to help other leaders of churches, or even having the humility to ask another church leaders for help. Churches walking with one another and carrying each other's load and diving into each other's mess. Not just a show of unity for a public gathering (although there is nothing wrong with that) but a deeply rooted unity built on a foundation of love and prayer behind the scenes.

And the more we do this the more the world will hunger for what we have. Jesus told us in John 17 that "the world" will testify to Jesus and will know him by our unity. By our *oneness*. Unity is a very effective form of evangelism, and it begins with our willingness to dive into the unclean and unclear mess of working with one another.

PAT BARRETT
HOUSEFIRES

THE WRONG QUESTION

I don't remember exactly when I learned there was something called a *denomination*. I think it wasn't until later in my life due to the fact that my dad's church (where he has been a pastor since I was four) was . . . how do I put this . . . eclectic. I don't know that many of my Baptist friends celebrated the Seder meal or recognized Yom Kippur. I actually recall one of the first times my dad picked me up from school wearing a yamaka. And I know what you're thinking . . . *Oh. I get it. He's Jewish.* The short answer is no. The complex answer is that he is actually a Lutheran meets Charismatic meets Catholic meets Jew.

Our church was diverse. Small but diverse. Many different denominations, many different perspectives, many different reasons why they didn't or shouldn't or couldn't fully get along. And yet they did. I mean, not always (of course). But the simple fact was, we shared something *together* that was far more powerful than anything we held *individually*.

Looking back, this is one of the most influential lessons I learned growing up: that we can be together even if we differ. Jesus seemed to believe this about people as well. I mean, seriously, look at the disciples that he chose. Mixing Jewish nationals and a tax collector. Or normal fishermen and the zealot. But for all their differences, they shared one thing in common: Jesus.

On some level, all of humanity understands this. Unless what we share together is more powerful than what we differ on, we will always champion *our own* cause. *Our own* ideas. *Our own* perspective. This may be an overgeneralization, and I'm sure there are exceptions to the idea, but deep down something rings true to this statement.

Perhaps it's because some of us have not experienced the breadth of thought that exists in the church today. Or maybe it's something deeper. Maybe it's because we all want to have Jesus on *our* side. I know I do! The only problem is that Scripture presents to us a bigger, broader, and more powerful story than the one we are *individually* a part of.

I love the story of Joshua getting ready to invade Jericho (Joshua 5:13–14). He has an encounter with the "commander of the army of the Lord" and asks him a familiar question we all seem to ask God at times: "Are you for us or for our enemies?" Are you on my side? Or their side? Is my cause the right one? Or is their cause the right one? Is my way of thinking correct? Or is their way of thinking correct?

The response is beautiful. The commander of the Lord's army says . . . *drum roll, please* . . . "Neither."

What?

Yes. "Neither."

That is a confusing response. But then again, maybe the response isn't the issue. Maybe Joshua was just asking the wrong question. It is possible that we can go our whole lives asking God the wrong questions.

"Are the Baptists right, or are the Lutherans right?"

"Are the Catholics right, or are the Pentecostals right?"

"Are the _____ right, or are the _____ right?" (You fill in the blanks.)

The real question may not be "Is God on *my* side?" but rather "Am I on *his* side?"

And even deeper questions: What if God sees the world in a different way than I do? And what if the story of his Spirit moving on the earth since the beginning of time is far more broad and powerful than just *my* denomination, *my* perspective, and *my* way of thinking?

The church has many different people with different perspectives. But in the end, it's the one thing we have in common—the one thing that we share—that brings us together. Jesus.

[6]

ONE MOVEMENT

From day one of OUTCRY we wanted to see the artists come together in a special way. We didn't want something flashy. When the artists met together before each night's event, we didn't want something big or polished. All of us were capable of that sort of thing, and we did it week in and week out—and we would soon be doing that before the thousands who were filling the arena. For us involved with OUTCRY, we wanted something approachable. Something that genuinely looked like the local church as we had all experienced. So we did what we knew. We decided to basically have a small group time. A time where each artist would take a night and lead acoustic worship and give a small devotional. I loved the idea and imagined it just falling into place. I mean, these are all amazing worship leaders from amazing churches. It would happen *easily*, right?

But as we began, our times together weren't at all what I imagined. In fact, they were a bit awkward and clunky. But we stayed committed to it, and night after night we would get together with an acoustic guitar and encourage one another. We'd sing worship songs we didn't all know. And we would do it without an overhead projector and sometimes with loud sound checks happening in the other room. But we plowed through them, and as we committed to the vision, we started to see something shift in the tour.

One night we asked if anybody was hearing anything from God in that moment. Kari Jobe raised her hand and said, "I think I have a prophetic word for Crowder. Is he in the room?" David was, and he raised his hand. Kari delivered a powerful and prophetic message to him. Then all of a sudden, Jenn Johnson from Bethel Music said, "Let's lay hands on David and his wife and pray." And as I looked around, I saw all of the people in the room surround David and pray. We came together the way I had seen in my mind. Like a small group. A group you would see at your church. In your town. We weren't trying to promote a new brand or movement. These nights didn't happen because of our work in OUTCRY. It was clearly an experience orchestrated by heaven for that moment. All we did was stay true to our vision, even when it didn't start off looking like we imagined it would. We were divinely stubborn.

Later on we looked back on *that* night as a real turning point in those small worship times. In fact, it was a turning point in the entire tour for me. There's something amazing that happens when leaders and influencers in the church come together and care for one another. Pray for one another. Even when there are no cameras around. Even when we're not live-tweeting about it. Just leaders behind the scenes caring for one another and lifting each other up to the Lord. There is something in that kind of unity that can be felt in the rest of the body. It doesn't have to be up front. It doesn't have to be on stage in front of a large group of people to be powerful.

> There's something amazing that happens when leaders and influencers in the church come together and care for one another.

It's the same for you and me. The small acts of unity and compassion for one another can shift the spiritual atmosphere of our church or neighborhood as well as our city or country. Unity isn't just reserved for the megachurch leaders or the large-platform worship leaders, it's for everyone to walk. In the big and small places in our lives. It's seen in us taking someone we disagree with out to lunch. It's evidenced in our reaching out to a leader we know who is having a difficult time. Maybe praying for the thriving ministry of someone whom you are secretly a bit jealous of. This is the unity that Jesus asked us to walk in. That we would love each other and do everything in our power to keep peace, friendship, and harmony with one another. And when this doesn't come easily, we need to take a step back and ask God for a little of *his* perspective.

MILE-HIGH VIEW

During the lead-up to the tour in 2015, I traveled a lot and spent time with many local church leaders around the country. On one of these trips I was looking out the window of my plane, watching the world go by, as we hit our cruising altitude of thirty-nine thousand feet. From that height everything starts to bleed together. You no longer view individual cars or notice individual houses. You simply see broad swatches of landscape going by. You can see clouds and mountains and horizons in a way you can't from the ground. You can view the beauty of the earth from a different, broader vantage point. It doesn't negate the beauty of the individual elements below. There is still beauty in an individual person. In the individual blooming flower or intricacies of a tiny insect. But as you pull back—out from the details of creation—you are able to see a *different* sort of beauty.

Shane and I are the guys with our heads in the clouds. We live at thirty-nine thousand feet. And that is the altitude at which OUTCRY was born. I love seeing the wide swatches of the church from a mile high and seeing a different image emerge.

During my traveling in this season and in my discussions with local church leaders, I have seen this image emerge. Something I have thought about often. Something I suspected but never *fully* saw until recently. As I travel the country, there is a clear sense that God is doing something *new* in the church. Something unexpected and very consequential. But it doesn't seem to be linked to a specific speaker, brand, or movement (not in the sense of *moment* as we've classically defined it). It isn't something that you can see unless you get up to cruising altitude.

There is a new season of church unity being unveiled unlike any we've seen in recent times. A oneness born at thirty-nine thousand feet. It is a "new" thing that is as ancient as the church itself, and you have to step back a bit to see it.

ONE

In the book of John, Jesus doesn't simply pray for the disciples. He also prays for all of those who will come after them. He prays for *us*. You and I right now. And his prayer is that we would be "one" in the same way that he and the Father are one.

> My prayer is not for them alone. I pray also for those who will believe in me through their message, that all of them may be one, Father, just as you are in me and I am in you. May they also be in us so that the world may believe that you have sent me. I have given them the glory that you gave me, that they may be one as we are one— I in them and you in me—so that they may be brought to complete unity. Then the world will know that you sent me and have loved them even as you have loved me. (John 17:20–23)

The heart of Jesus for his children is that they'd see they are on the same team. He prayed for a oneness in our *identity* with him. A oneness in spirit so strong it would mirror his connection to the Father. He didn't pray for oneness in personality. He didn't ask that we would all have the same gifting or convictions.

I think many times we imagine unity being built on a foundation of agreement. That kind of unity can't happen until we all see the world in the same way. Until we carry all of the same social or theological convictions. But we build this assumption based on the detailed opinions that we see up close.

Just as an artist who steps back from his painting to get a true view of his work, we need to take a step back to clearly see the spirit of unity that God is pouring out on his people. Today. Right now.

I see it increasing all around the world.

The unity that God is pouring out is not found in a common set of theological points. It isn't that we all care about the same issues. God is not calling us to *sameness* but to unity. Loving one another not simply in spite of our differences but *because* of our differences.

Cyprian was a Christian leader and writer in the third century. He once said,

Although the church of Jesus Christ is found in many different places, she is one church, not many. After all, there are many rays of sunlight, but only one sun. A tree has many boughs, each slightly different from others, but all drawing their strength from one source. Many streams may flow down a hillside, but they all originate from the same spring. In exactly the same way each local congregation belongs to the one true church.

I think this beautifully communicates the heart of God for his bride. Many streams flowing from one source. We are running down *one* hill toward *one* destiny. Some of us carry more water. Some of us wind around more obstacles than others. But we all lead to the same place, and in the end we will flow together into one pool.

It's not that we in the church are the same. It's not that we need to work with *every* church to be unified. Unity is happening and will increase as time goes on. Not because we want it badly enough. Not because of our efforts. But because Jesus prayed for it. And the words of Jesus are powerful things.

MAKE EVERY EFFORT

So does all of this mean that we simply sit back and *wait* for unity to happen? Isn't there *some* role that you and I play?

Make every effort to keep the unity of the Spirit through the bond of peace. There is one body and

one Spirit, just as you were called to one hope
when you were called; one Lord, one faith, one
baptism; one God and Father of all, who is over
all and through all and in all. (Ephesians 4:3–6)

Paul dumps a lot of theological meat about the
church in this passage. He says there *is one* body and *one*
spirit. He says we are called to *one* hope. That our oneness comes by Jesus and though Jesus. There is a oneness
to the body that God places on us despite our differences.

But he begins by saying we should "make every
effort" to maintain unity through peace. We are called to
try everything we can to stay connected. When a local
church is filled with people making every effort to keep
the "bond of peace," the power of Christ is magnified
through them. Not simply an invisible camaraderie but
an active and relational connection with one another.
But this takes effort, grace, and humility.

In his book *Your Church Is Too Small*, John H.
Armstrong discusses this sort of relational unity and the
role we have to play in it. He says, "If Jesus is praying for
a oneness we already possess, then this prayer has nothing to do with what we should be doing right now. Just
ask yourself a simple question: Why would Jesus pray for
something that is already true? Why does he pray for us

to be brought to complete unity if it is something that we already possess?"

That is the question. So, will we see a perfect unity in the church one day? Yes, because Jesus prayed for it. Do we have it yet? No, because Jesus prayed for it.

We are to make *every effort*, in and through the spheres of influence we have, to unite with other believers through the common bond and mission of Jesus. This is his will and our mission, and it's a source of joy when carried out. So in your small group, make every effort. In your family, make every effort. In your church, make every effort. In your city, from church to church, make every effort. Pastor to pastor, make every effort. I think we get it.

As the old cliché goes, unity begins with U-N-I. It isn't a magical formula. It may not feel significant. It won't feel earth-shattering when you apologize to your friend. Or take that other pastor out to coffee. It will feel small. But the beautiful thing about Jesus is that there is significance in the small. In the things we feel are inconsequential, he finds beauty and power.

PERSPECTIVE SHIFT

There have been times and seasons historically when the church pulled together. Where leaders would advocate for different factions coming together as one. These are called—we're going to get real fancy here—*ecumenical movements*. Times when Christians were challenged to put aside their differences and work together. The challenge comes when setting aside differences involves whittling down theology to the most essential pieces. But the word *essential* has as many different definitions as there are people trying to define it!

Now this is a place where you can find yourself in a sticky situation. How do we know what is essential? What truths in the Bible do we have to sacrifice for the name of unity?

Before we paint ourselves into the proverbial theological corner, let's go back to a couple of things. First, let's not define unity as *sameness*. There is true diversity in the church, and this is beautiful. Let's consider unity through this lens. Next, let's go way back to our discussion on *expectations*. If our expectation is that unity is only possible when factions are completely dissolved and we are humming along in complete theological and relational harmony, we will be sorely disappointed. This is where we get caught up in the definitions of indefinable words like *essential*.

So if unity is not sameness and will never be perfect, where do we go from here?

Ultimately the unity of the church begins with a shift in perspective. Taking a step back to view God's church through his eyes. To see the broad landscape from thirty-nine thousand feet above. To see the beauty and unity of the church from a height that causes details and differences to blur a little. C. S. Lewis once said, "When all is said (and truly said) about the divisions of Christendom, there remains, by God's mercy, an enormous common ground."

> Our natural instinct is to dive into the details and find our differences. But God sees us as more than our theological, political, or philosophical stances.

We have more common ground than we can see. Will there be serious theological differences for us to discuss? Always. But do we have more in common under the banner and identification of Jesus than we think? Absolutely. Our natural instinct is to dive into the details and find our differences. But God sees us as more than our theological, political, or philosophical stances. He sees us. He sees his church. His bride. His body. He sees us in a context we will never see unless we ask for it.

If you care a lot about the details of theology, more power to you! I actually love talking theology and details as much as the next guy. I have many friends whom I love and admire who live for it. But we can't make that the cornerstone of our unity. There is just too much diversity in this messy, worldwide movement called the church for it to be neatly packaged and defined.

ONE RIVER

Martin Smith has a way of putting things in perspective. A way of making things simple out of the complicated. He joined us in our second OUTCRY tour, and he and his amazing family added more than I can communicate here. He poured into everyone around him and had a huge impact on the tour—and on me personally. One evening he played the song, "Did You Feel the Mountains Tremble," which was a lightning bolt of inspiration to me—especially the lines that say the church will one day cause the darkness to tremble . . .

> When all the saints join in one song.
> And all the streams flow as one river

To catch a vision of all of the streams coming together and flowing as one river is a beautiful picture of what God did—and still does—in his church. There are many streams in the church that seem to wander and wind on their own. But again, when you change your perspective—go to a higher vantage point—you see them all coming together. They are moving in the same direction and have the same destination.

OUTCRY IS NOT A MOVEMENT

When Shane and I started OUTCRY, we came up with a couple of ground rules:

First, OUTCRY will always be spelled in all capitals because . . . why not?! Chalk it up to an artistic choice in branding. Not everything has to be seeped in meaning. I say, if it looks good do it! Anyway, I digress.

Second—which isn't second at all—is that we are never to be referred to internally as a "movement." We have had new social media people come in and post on Facebook or Twitter, "Outcry is a movement that . . ." Other than the lowercase letters—which irks me just to type them—the word *movement* must promptly be removed! We immediately jump to our cell phone and correct the egregious mistake. But why? Lots of amazing ministries that we love use that word. What's the big deal?

For us, OUTCRY is all about *the* movement. We are all about Jesus and his church. We don't believe that we are the new, trendy club that you need to sign up for. We don't believe that we will be around forever—I know, not exactly a motivating speech for our team! But we won't.

There is only *one* movement under the sun that will be around forever. One movement Jesus wraps his identity around. And the church is not a collection of movements—it is *the* movement. Its success does not rise and fall with its "cool" factor. It doesn't rely on the greatness of a few people—as movements of the world often do. No! Our movement—his movement—will be around for the rest of eternity! And in light of that, we emphatically say we are not a movement.

As we get more of that perspective inside of us, the more we begin to see the unity that Jesus prayed for come to pass. We aren't simply a collection of factions that need to find common ground. No, we are an amazingly diverse movement that looks different all around the globe, and we find our connection under the banner of Jesus, who freely gave himself over for our freedom. It's a beautiful thing that has never been seen on this scale in all of history. He gave himself over for our movement. For his people.

This is so central to our philosophy at OUTCRY that we would not see each other as people who need to be the same but as people who need to champion one another in our differences.

This is where unity begins. In a simple plane ride over the story of the church. A shift in perspective so we can see one another in the light of this beautiful and complicated work of art called the church. Once we see that, our future begins to look bright. And we begin to *truly* believe that our best days are ahead.

CHRIS LLEWELLYN
REND COLLECTIVE

THE PEOPLE

We had finished the last note of the song, but every hand was still in the air. Every eye was closed. We had sung with all our might, and the sweetness of God's presence was heavy in the room. It was beautiful.

To clarify, it *was* beautiful . . . until suddenly, in the middle of that holy moment, a voice came over the speakers from the front of the small room.

"Uhh . . . Diane needs a lift to the airport on Monday. Is there anyone in the church who can help with this?"

I can't help but laugh a little when I remember this moment.

It was obviously jarring at the time, to be ripped out of a "worship" moment into the stark reality of the needs around me. Oddly enough, though, this has become one of my favorite stories from church. As time has gone by,

I've come to realize that I'd merely been moved from one expression of worship to another equally valid one. Both singing and service rising together as an offering pleasing unto the Lord.

Jesus distills the Ten Commandments into this single expression: love God and love your neighbor. This memory paints that picture so well. The more I reflect on these commands, the more I realize they're not different at all. One is merely a symptom of the other. Whenever we fall more in love with the Father, we fall more in love with the people he's made in his image. And whenever we act in love toward our neighbors, we see traces of the God who made them and fall more in love with him.

This simple command sums up who God is, both immanent and transcendent. Both God on a throne and a baby in a manger. He's concerned with the big picture and the tiny details.

When we try to love God but lose sight of our neighbor, that's when cold and mean religion begins. If we're only concerned about our fellow man and never look to God, we'll lose the resource we need to actually love the world—the Holy Spirit. At best, we'll be a social club full of nice people. Simply being nice is not a fruit of the Spirit, but being wildly good is evidence of his presence in our lives.

We love musical worship because it feels good. That's

why we go to concerts, learn how to play the guitar, and attend conferences. It isn't evil but is actually restoring to our souls and commanded by God. But for the health of the church, we need to be ready to be shaken out of our comfort level for the service of others—even if it is jarring. Because it all falls under the heading of *worship*.

My parents' generation used to have a saying that said something like this: "You're so heavenly minded, you're of no earthly use." But my charge to the church is to be so heavenly minded that we can't help but be of earthly use.

[7]

OUR STORY

've had people ask, "So how do you define the local church?" I think this is an important question, but there is a reason I've waited till the last chapter of this book to talk about it. It is a process that can paint you into a corner pretty quickly! But up till now, I think we've established the *identity* of the church (chapter 3) and have established that the church itself is diverse, messy and—often times—very difficult to define in a concise way. But for the sake of clarity, let's try!

So the natural, churchy place to start is in the original language. The word most often used in the New Testament is the Greek word *Ekklesia*. The simple definition of *Ekklesia* is an assembly or congregation. It also carries the idea of being called out or called forth from one place to another. The assembly of the called-out ones.

Now, in the context of how the word is used, it also has a *universal* connotation. Meaning the word *church*— or *Ekklesia*—is being used to describe the sum of all the diverse parts. This is where we get the word *catholic*. For us, the word catholic is a certain sect of Christianity. We see it through a particular theological or cultural lens, but the *catholic* church simply means the *universal* church. So in this sense, when Paul discusses "the church," he is not being super specific. It is a broad and universal use of the word.

This means the church is larger than the box you and I may try to put it into. There are certain theological ideas that are hot-button issues today—you can probably think of three right now!—that are ultimately more *cultural* and *political* than foundational elements of the church. Trying to define the church by these would be, in my humble opinion, not a great place to start.

So let's start somewhere basic:

If you declare with your mouth, "Jesus is Lord," and believe in your heart that God raised him from the dead, you will be saved. For it is with your heart that you believe and are justified, and it is with your mouth that you profess your faith and are saved. (Romans 10:9)

According to Paul, it is in the *believing* of your heart in the redeeming actions of Jesus that brings the *justification* of God. It is the profession of Jesus that brings the saving nature of the gospel.

So ultimately we are left with some crucial questions: Are you defined by the redemption found through the life, death, and resurrection of Jesus? Do you believe He is Lord? Have you been called out of the world and into his kingdom? If the answer is yes, then welcome to the *Ekklesia!*

These are the basics. The church has many different people from many cultural backgrounds but—as my friend Pat Barrett said earlier—we have this one crucial thing in common: Jesus. And if you find your heart believing in him and your mouth confessing him, then you are in. If your life is defined by Jesus, then you and I are working together in this world-changing, history-altering movement called the church.

We love to make this more complicated than it is. In fact, what we often see in the church is a law of thermodynamics called entropy. Entropy is the force of nature that pulls us from order to chaos. From simple to complicated. It is the force that causes ants to create more and more intricate tunnels the longer they are at it. Or that causes more and more laws and complications to be established in a government structure. It is also the force that causes us to add more and more theological complication to a simple gospel. And it doesn't take long to walk away from the simplicity of Jesus's love and redemption. The church in Ephesus was dealing with it within a generation of Jesus.

In the book of Revelation, we read a prophetic word from the Lord being delivered to the church in Ephesus. It starts out nice enough. God is generally pleased with the actions of the church. He sees that its people are enduring hardship with a triumphant and abundant strength. They are running the race and not growing weary. Pretty great, right? They are doing a lot of *things* right. But God's message takes a twist.

> Yet I hold this against you: You have forsaken the love you had at first. Consider how far you have fallen! Repent and do the things you did at first. (2:4–5)

They have forgotten the basis of their faith. The first love of God. The first love of the gospel. We can do and believe a lot of different things, but we should never forsake the common bond we all have in the gospel.

Yes, there are important theological points that are worth discussing under this umbrella, but not in this book. We can always find a thousand reasons why we should segregate theologically. But we have more in common than we believe when we are defined by the lordship and leadership of Jesus.

Under this banner, let's consider one another highly. Let's take time to focus on the amazing things he is doing around the world though his people. Let's take time to see each other as a family, rooting for one another, championing the different gifts each of us brings to the table.

Let's come around our common story. The story that Jesus has been weaving for thousands of years and is bringing to completion. We have walked—though only a few baby steps—through the amazing history of the church. We've had ups and

> We can always find a thousand reasons why we should segregate theologically. But we have more in common than we believe when we are defined by the lordship and leadership of Jesus.

downs. Our story can bring us together and our love for one another can now testify to the world about the saving nature of our God. But we have not only a common past and present—we have a common future. A day coming that will make all other major times in our history seem small in comparison. There are amazing days ahead for the church, which gives us a hope for today. A hope that brings in focus all of our past and present. And we don't have to guess at his plans. God has already told us what it will look like.

SPOILER ALERT

Do you have *that* friend? That person who loves their football team. Their basketball team. Their Olympic curling team. That person who will drag you into a random sports bar or restaurant to watch his team. Or even worse . . . that friend who drags you into a random sports bar or restaurant to watch the *rival* of his favorite team. Just in pure hopes of seeing the enemy's utter demise. Roll Tide! War Eagle! Fight On! Or—in my case—Bear Down! Is your friend's name Shane? Mine is. And the aforementioned situation may or may not have involved him.

But what if this friend couldn't see the game *but* was recording it at home? What would he say? "Don't tell me the score! Please, don't tell me how it ends!" What do we say before we tell someone the end of a movie? "Spoiler alert!" We feel we must alert people to the fact that telling them how the story ends will literally spoil the experience. In the world of entertainment, knowing how it ends ruins the process of getting there. If you know who wins in the end, it ruins the experience of the game or story along the way.

But in the story of God, we *do* know the end. God tells us his story from Genesis to Revelation. We know how the story started. We know the middle (we're living it). And we know *the end.* But in our case, God knows that we need to know the end of *this* story. Unlike the entertainment of a movie or sports game that lasts a couple of hours, we are in the story of God and his people that lasts millennia.

Knowing how the story ends colors how we view the here and now. We tend to look at the story told in Revelation through a *personal* lens. "How does Revelation affect *me*? What will *I* experience in heaven? What will heaven look like?" But we seem to gloss over the implications it has on *us.*

Many times I have missed something significant in the Bible by simply trying to look too hard at the details. Sometimes God gives a significant revelation or insight in the *simple,* obvious pieces of Scripture.

A NEW WHITE GARMENT

The book of Revelation has plenty of details that can distract us. There are many interpretations and lots of staunch stances that lead to many different camps and theologies with extra fancy names. Eschatologically speaking these camps include, but are not limited to, premillennial dispensationalism, amillennial, or postmillennial. Perhaps you are more of a post-tribulation pre-millennialist. Or maybe you are more of a mid-tribulation amillennialist. However you slice it, there are myriads of different opinions the deeper you go.

But for these verses in Revelation 19, I don't want to focus on the details. I don't want us to self-divide into camps just for one moment. Let's not discuss who is *invited* versus who is theologically considered *in* "the bride" group. Let's focus on the *moment*.

Then I heard what sounded like a great multitude, like the roar of rushing waters and like loud peals of thunder, shouting: "Hallelujah! For our Lord God Almighty reigns. Let us rejoice and be glad and give him glory! For the wedding of the Lamb has come, and his bride has made herself ready. Fine linen, bright and clean, was given her to wear." (Fine linen stands for the righteous acts of God's holy people.) Then the angel said to me, "Write this: Blessed are those who are invited to the wedding supper of the Lamb!" And he added, "These are the true words of God." (Revelation 19:6–9)

Forgive me as I embark on a little artistic embellishment and interpretation.

The *bride* is ready. She is clothed in a new white garment. All of the *righteous acts* of the body of Christ are made manifest, and she can officially drape it over herself, covering every flaw and sense of self-consciousness. Her dress is new, dazzlingly bright white and made of the finest quality. She looks beautiful. She becomes everything she was designed to be in a single moment. And standing before her is the bridegroom. Jesus. Though time is not a limitation to him, he still carries a sense of expectancy and joy over this moment. There is a roar from the crowd as she enters. It is so expansive with attendees that the crowd sounds like a raging river. Like great peals of thunder. An explosion of joyful noise so loud that it shakes your bones and awakens your soul. It is an awe-inspiring moment of pure power unlike anything witnessed by mankind. The greatest moments in history and the largest gatherings of people pale in comparison. A *new* history in a new heaven and new earth are being written.

This is the culmination of the entirety of church history. From Jesus walking the earth to the explosive moments in Acts 2. From the persecution of the church to this triumphant moment where she becomes all she was meant to be. And this is the future of our story, the future of the church. All of it added together. The church you and I are a part of week after week. Even the churches that seem tired and old. The churches that seem to some as insignificant or out of touch. House churches. Megachurches. All of them wrapped up into this single scene in Revelation, where the bride walks into the destiny that God had planned for her since the dawn of creation.

Here is the spoiler alert to our story: the church is *still* around in Revelation 19. "Some spoiler alert" you may say, "I already knew that." But do you *know* it? Deep down do you carry the pride of knowing that you are on the winning team?

Don't miss this through the details of theology. Theology is a beautiful thing, but occasionally you need to step back so you don't miss the forest through the trees.

REMEMBER

As OUTCRY was gearing up in 2015, I was traveling the country doing radio interviews. Many times—as I quickly learned—I had to give a sort of pre-interview interview. While prepping for an interview in Atlanta I received one of these pre-interview calls. The questions addressed the usual subjects: how the tour started, who was going to be there, etc. But as the rhythm of the interview began to slow, the interviewer changed her tone.

"So," she asked, "you say you support the local church, but how do you *really* support it? Are you guys training anyone? Are you providing financial support of some kind? How do you *practically* support the church?"

These are the right-between-the-eyes sort of questions. I could hear her probing with a healthy dose of skepticism, and deep down somewhere I froze. My mind started going a mile a minute. This was an obvious question that I should have thought through at some point. I thought, *How are we doing that? We need to talk about doing this better. Why haven't I thought of this one?*

Out of the chaos of my thoughts, it came back to me. We *had* thought of this, and I had the perfect answer: "That is not what OUTCRY is about. We don't want to come into your city and tell you how to do church better.

There are a million excellent resources out there for that. We are coming to remind the church of who she is. That the church is the most amazing movement the world has ever seen. To remind her that she has a rich past and a glorious future."

And this is another important aspect of OUTCRY. We don't want to come into your city and tell you how to do church better. We want to bring encouragement to the discouraged. We want you to remember how great your church is and how great *the* church is. We don't want you to leave any of our events feeling defeated. Like you need our stage or lights or wisdom in order for your church to be more effective. We want to remind you that no matter how small your church is, it is part of the story that culminates—and some may argue, truly *begins*—in Revelation. It has a truly *glorious* future.

OPEN EYES AND HEARTS

Sometimes God reminds us that *he* is in charge. God is not beholden to political or cultural rules. His plans don't have to make sense to anyone. God is wild, and ultimately he will—as he says in Isaiah—*do what he pleases*: "I make known the end from the beginning, from ancient times, what is still to come. I say, 'My purpose will stand, and I will do all that I please'" (46:10).

I've had many times where God has crashed my paradigm and reminded me that I'm in the middle of a story that has been going on for thousands of years. There will be *some* plot twists as we approach the end of the story.

One day I was sitting in a staff meeting at church when all of a sudden I felt as if I were being awakened. As if I had plunged myself into a cold bath, my senses immediately awakened to a new idea that crashed my paradigm. Our church is a pretty classic, non-denominational church. Our pastor, Mark Buckley, is a seasoned leader who started his ministry in the Jesus movement of the 1970s. He is a wise and discerning guy who knows the Bible inside and out. He is someone I trust theologically when he exposes me to a ministry. So as I sat there and heard about a Catholic unity meeting happening at our church, I felt extremely intrigued.

For the entirety of my Christian life, I've only heard the theological differences between Catholics and non-denominational Protestant churches. I never felt actively opposed to Catholics, but I was certainly aware of their theological points with which I disagreed—and fairly strongly at that. But as I sat and listened, my heart began to soften, and God began to speak to me. I began to hear amazing stories. Stories of Charismatic Catholic awakenings in South America. Stories of the Spirit of God breaking out over many different Catholic congregations all over the world. Stories of local Catholic Cardinals attending evangelical worship events and approaching the stage for prayer. Amazing and clearly God-ordained moments of unity were taking place at an increasingly fast rate all over the world. And it got my attention.

This organization was a mixture of Charismatic Catholics and evangelical leaders who would put together worship services that looked very much like what I experienced on a Sunday morning at our church. Fittingly, they were named John 17. On top of all the things happening through their ministry, they got the attention of the Pope himself, who encouraged them through notes and even by filming videos for them.

Now, do I still have theological differences with Catholics? Yes. But as I listened to their heart and the stories where God was moving, I began to see past those. This is one of those moments that widened my horizon. It broke my paradigm of what God could do, and it widened my view of the church significantly. Not only this, but we are at the five-hundred-year anniversary of the Reformation. This may or may not be significant, but God is doing something new in this season that makes that number seem noteworthy to me! He continues to open doors and break down barriers of separation, and it truly brings to life the words of Jesus when he said, "*Whoever has ears, let them hear.*"

WHAT'S COMING?

There is something different in the air. We can all feel it. It isn't simply political or cultural change. It isn't just related to the things we can see. God is doing something massive in the church, which you and I are just beginning to see. It begins with us seeing the church differently. Seeing each other differently. And seeing our past, present, and future differently.

Every night of OUTCRY we say this one line: "How can the church be dying if it cannot die?" When we read Revelation 19, everything in our being told us this was a *true* revelation for our time. It is a simple phrase and idea, but it is a sign of the times of what is coming in the church.

These days more and more people are talking about unity in the body of Christ. More and more people are beginning to see that the church is an amazing thing to be a part of. The way churches operate may change. Styles of music will ebb and flow. Maybe it's a season of house churches shifting into liturgical structure in services.

Maybe the megachurch movement plateaus. Maybe it doesn't. In the end, Jesus will have his way with the church no matter what form it is in. It will continue to move toward the power seen in Revelation 19. We won't see the fullness of what she can become until she puts that new white garment on. But until that day we must be diligent about what's in front of us. We need to encourage those around us and dive into the messy but beautiful struggle we call the local church.

Our movement—the movement of Jesus—is something to be proud of. Something for us to stand with. It doesn't find its worth politically. It doesn't find its worth through public opinion. It finds its worth from the one who loves it like his own body. It finds its worth in the indescribable, beautiful, and frighteningly powerful Son of God. Jesus spoke us into being. The same voice that spoke galaxies and time into being. The same voice that can shake the entirety of creation with his voice. He spoke our movement into being.

> **Jesus spoke us into being. The same voice that spoke galaxies and time into being. The same voice that can shake the entirety of creation with his voice. He spoke our movement into being.**

The best days of the church are ahead of us. The moment we grasp the significance of *our* church—in the local, here-and-now sense—will be the moment we walk in power and freedom right where we are. The moment we begin to see each other as members of the same family, our influence will spread. Not viewing one another as competition. Not simply seeing the areas of theological disagreement when we look at each other, but seeing other churches with the eyes of Jesus. With eyes of great grace, love, and camaraderie. We all have our own strengths and weaknesses. But together we create a beautiful and diverse tapestry. Together we become louder to the world around us.

This is what's coming. In fact, it's already here. We just need to pause and open our eyes to see it.

The next big thing is here. It's always been here.

NOTES

1. https://livinginliminality.files.wordpress.com/2009/03/aris_report_2008.pdf
2. http://www.newsweek.com/meacham-end-christian-america-77125
3. http://www.cnn.com/2015/05/12/living/pew-religion-study/
4. http://www.pewforum.org/2015/05/12/americas-changing-religious-landscape/
5. http://www.huffingtonpost.com/byron-williams/christianity-has-only-itself-to
   -blame-for-its-demise_b_7546058.html
6. http://www.ccel.org/ccel/feltoe/dionysius.dionysius.letters.e14.html
7. http://www.npr.org/sections/thesalt/2013/11/03/242359207/5-things-you-might
   -not-have-known-about-god-and-beer
8. Eric Metaxas, *Amazing Grace: William Wilberforce and the Heroic Campaign to End Slavery* (San Francisco: HarperOne, 2007), xiii–xiv, xvi.

ABOUT THE AUTHOR

Ryan Romeo is an artist, worship leader, writer, and speaker. He has a deep passion for the church and all things creative. He currently works at his local church and is the Creative Director for the OUTCRY Tour. He lives in Phoenix, AZ, with his wife, Blake, and their three children.

IF YOU ENJOYED THIS BOOK, WILL YOU CONSIDER SHARING THE MESSAGE WITH OTHERS?

Mention the book in a blog post or through Facebook, Twitter, Pinterest, or upload a picture through Instagram.

Recommend this book to those in your small group, book club, workplace, and classes.

Head over to facebook.com/OUTCRYtour, "LIKE" the page, and post a comment as to what you enjoyed the most.

Tweet "I recommend reading #OUTCRYbook by @RyanRomeo of @OUTCRY_tour // @worthypub"

Pick up a copy for someone you know who would be challenged and encouraged by this message.

Write a book review online.

Visit us at worthypublishing.com

twitter.com/worthypub

worthypub.tumblr.com

facebook.com/worthypublishing

pinterest.com/worthypub

instagram.com/worthypub

youtube.com/worthypublishing

CYBERPUNKS

CYBERFREEDOM

CHANGE REALITY SCREENS

by Timothy Leary

RONIN

Berkeley, CA

Timothy Leary
Fugitive Philosopher
CyberPunk Time Traveler

CYBERPUNKS

CYBERFREEDOM

CHANGE REALITY SCREENS

by Timothy Leary

CyberPunks CyberFreedom
Change Reality Screens

Copyright 2008: The Futique Trust
ISBN: 978-1-57951-084-8

Published by
Ronin Publishing, Inc.
PO Box 22900
Oakland, CA 94609
www.roninpub.com

Production:

Editor:	Beverly A. Potter, Ph.D. *docpotter.com*
Cover Design:	Brian Groppe *BrianGroppe.com*
Book Design:	Beverly A. Potter

Fonts:

Big Cheese light and dark—Emigre
Century Schoolbook—Monotype
ITC Machine—Adobe Systems/Linotype
Univers—Adobe Systems

Library of Congress Card Number: 2008931384
Distributed to the book trade by **PGW/Perseus**
Printed in the United States by **Data Repro**

Derived from *Chaos & Cyber Culture*.

RONIN BOOKS FOR INDEPENDENT MINDS

by Timothy Leary

High Priest

Chaos & Cyber Culture

The Politics of Ecstasy

Psychedelic Prayers

Change Your Brain

The Politics of Self-Determination

Start Your Own Religion

Your Brain Is God

Turn On Tune In Drop Out

Musings on Human Metamorphoses

Evolutionary Agents

The Politics of PsychoPharmacology

The Fugitive Philosopher

IS THERE
A LIFE
AFTER
YOUTH?

Think for Yourself
Change Your Reality Screen

TABLE OF CONTENTS

You are only as old as the last time you changed your mind. I changed my mind often.

Reboot Your Brain!

THE ETERNAL PHILOSOPHY OF CHAOS

For several thousand years it has seemed obvious that the basic nature of the universe is extreme complexity, inexplicable disorder—that mysterious, tangled magnificence popularly known as Chaos. The poetic Hindus believed the universe was a dreamy dance of illusion that they called *maya*. The paradoxical, psychological Buddhists spoke of a void too complex—maybe a trillion times too complex—to be grasped by the human A-B-C-1-2-3 word-processing system—the mind.

Chinese poet-philosopher Lao-tzu sardonically reminded us that the *tao* is forever changing complexities at light speed, elusive and inaccessible to our fingers and thumbs laboriously tapping letters on our alphanumeric keyboards and mind-operating systems.

Individualistic thinking is the original sin of the Judo-Christian-Islamic Bibles. It sabotages attempts by the authorities to order Chaos.

> **Law-and-order systems trivialize and demonize the dangerous concepts of Self—individual aims and personal knowledge. Thinking for Your Self is heretical, treasonous, blasphemous.**

Socrates, that proud, self-reliant Athenian democrat, indiscreetly blurted out the dangerous secret when he said, *"The aim of human life is to know thy self."* This is surely the most subversive T-shirt flaunted over the centuries by humanists, the most confrontational bumper sticker on their neuro-auto-mobiles.

The first rule of every law-and-order system is to trivialize and demonize the dangerous concepts of Self—individual aims and personal knowledge. Thinking for Your Self is heretical, treasonous, blasphemous. Only devils and satans do it. Creative thinking, committed out loud, becomes a capital crime. It was "Three Strikes and You're Out" for several hundred thousand Protestant dissenters during the Inquisitions of the Roman papacy—not to forget the witch burnings performed by the Protestants when they took charge of the Chaos control department.

It was all very simple to the law-and-order controllers. There are the immortal Gods and Goddesses up there in that Gated Community on Olympus Drive. And then there are us—meaningless mortals, slaving around down here in the low-rent flatlands.

The concept of individuals with choice and identity seemed total folly, the ultimate nightmare—not just of authoritarian bureaucrats, but of common-sense liberals. Chaos must be controlled!

The standard way to tame and domesticate the impossible complexity that surrounds us is to invent a few "tooth-fairy" Gods, the more infantile the better, and to lay down a few childish rules: Honor your father and your mother, etc. The rules are simple and logical. You passively obey. You pray. You sacrifice. You work. You believe.

And then, Praise the Bored, let there be no terrorizing notions about individuals hanging around this meaningless, disordered universe trying to figure how to design themselves into individual selves.

Chaos Engineering

 The first Chaos engineers may have been the Hindu sages who designed a method for operating the brain called yoga. The Buddhists produced one of the great hands-on do-it-yourself manuals for operating the brain: *The Tibetan Book of the Dying.* Chinese Taoists developed the teaching of going with the flow—not clinging to idea-structures, but changing and evolving. The message was: Be cool. Don't panic. Chaos is good. Chaos creates infinite possibilities.

The wacko Socratic idea of Do It Yourself (D.I.Y.), which created modern democracy, was a

The first Chaos engineers may have been the Hindu sages who designed a method for operating the brain called yoga.

practical, common sense, sassy Athenian version of the Hindu Buddhist Taoist yogas. And remember where this foolishness got Tibet? Know-where!

The most dangerous idea is this crazed, megalomaniac Socratic notion of KNOW which defines the serf-human being as a thinker. Outrageous impudence! The slave is encouraged to become a philosopher! The serf strives to be a psychologist! A potential yogic sage!

This heresy predicts why later atheist evolutionists like Linnesus and Darwin defined our super chimp species as *Femina (Homo) sapiens.*

> Chinese Taoists developed the teaching of going with the flow—not clinging to idea-structures, but changing and evolving. The message was: Be cool. Don't panic. Chaos is good. Chaos creates infinite possibilities.

The Chaos Without

For centuries there existed a fanatic taboo against scientific understanding. Why? Because of the fear of Chaos. The facts about our (apparently) insignificant place in the galactic dance are so insulting to the control freaks who try—so manfully and diligently and seriously—to manage Chaos that they forbade any intelligent attempts to look out there and dig the glorious complexity.

At one point consciousness altering devices like the microscope and telescope were criminalized for exactly the same reasons that psychedelic plants were banned in later times. They allow us to peer into bits and zones of Chaos.

Galileo got busted and Bruno got the Vatican microwave for showing that the Sun did not circle the Earth. Religious and political Chaosphobes naturally want the nice, tidy, comfy universe to cuddle around them.

In the last century science has developed technical extensions of the human sensorium that specify the truly spooky nature of the complexities we inhabit.

Stellar astronomy describes a universe of fantastic multiplicity: a hundred billion tiny star systems in our tiny galaxy, a hundred billion galaxies in our teeny universe.

The Chaos Within

 In the last decades of the 20th Century, scientists began to study the complexity within the human brain.

Talk about Chaos! It turns out that the brain is a galactic network of a hundred billion neurons. Each neuron is an information system as complex as a mainframe computer. Each neuron is connected to ten thousand other neurons. Each of us is equipped with a universe of neurocomplexity that is inscrutable to our alphanumeric minds.

This brain power is at once the most humiliating fact about our current ignorance, and the most thrilling prospect of our potential divinity— once we start learning how to operate our brain.

The Navigational Game Plan

Chaos theory allows us to appreciate our assignments: the understanding, enjoyment, and celebration of the delightful nature of the whole universe—including the totally mad paradoxes within our brains.

Activating the so-called right brain eliminates one of the last taboos against understanding Chaos and provides a hands-on scientific basis for the philosophy of humanism—encouraging us to team up with others to design our own personal versions of Chaos.

During the Roaring 20th Century,

the equations for quantum physics

led to the development of

quantum appliances that

allowed humans

to receive, process,

and transmit electronic images.

2

HOW I BECAME AN AMPHIBIAN

I n 1980, Ronald Reagan, a screen person, became the president of the United States. At the same time, the screen image of an Iranian mullah, the leader of a notoriously irritable fundamentalist sect, became the rallying point of the Islamic world. In the same year, surveys showed that the average American spent more than four hours a day neuronarcotized by the artificial realities and fake news dramas on television screens—more time than is spent on any other waking activity in the flesh-material reality.

It was about then that I too found myself mutating gradually, imperceptibly, into an amphibious form. The word "amphibian" comes from the Greek *amphi*—double, and *bios*—life.

I began spending around four hours a day producing and scripting and directing the images on my personal screen. Some of these digitized words and images were my own. Some were encoded on disks. Others were phoned to me by friends and colleagues at almost the speed of light.

In this way I learned how to file, process, organize, clarify, store, retrieve, and transmit my digitized thoughts in the form of words and icons.

These exercises in translating thoughts to digital codes and screen images have helped me understand how my brain works, how the universe evolves in terms of information algorithms. And, in the most practical mode, to understand:

1. How we can avoid television dictatorships, and

2. How we can democratize the cyberscreen politics of the future.

My experiences, far from being original or unique, seem to be part of an enormous cultural metamorphosis. Like millions of others, I came to feel as comfortable in Cyberia, Tubeland, on the other side of my electronic-reality window, as I do operating in the closed-in Terrarium of the material world. My brain, like yours, needs to be clothed in cyberwear and to swim, float, navigate through the oceans of electronic data.

Surely we can be forgiven if we are confused by all this. Organisms in the process of metamorphosis are forced to use the metaphors of past stages in order to anticipate future stages—an obviously risky business. "They'll never get me up in one of those," says the caterpillar to the butterfly.

"They'll never get me up in one of those," says the caterpillar to the butterfly.

From Aquaria to Terrarium to Cyberia

In our early marine forms, we lived under water. Trapped in Aquaria, we could peer up through the sea ceiling and sense a wide world up there.

In the Devonian period—400 million years ago—we started developing the technology needed to migrate to the shoreline. I am talking state-of-the-art terra wear: skin-tight dry suits to maneuver around in the land world. Thus we became amphibians, able to live both in Aquaria and in Terrarium.

During the Thassic period we evolved to the mammalian stage and lost our ability to inhabit Aquaria. For the last 225 million years, we mammals crawled and ran around the Earth's surface, nervously improving our Terrarium survival technologies.

Then, during the last million or so years, human beings developed enormous brains that we did not know how to operate. Our hairless primate ancestors—banded in social groups, living in caves, fashioning clubs to fight tigers—were equipped with the same brain model that we are just now learning how to operate.

And for thousands of years, the more poetic or neurologically advanced among us have gazed upward on starry nights, beginning to realize that another universe exists in space and that we are trapped in the Terrarium of Earth's surface. Or what's a heaven for?

Around 1900, physicists like Einstein and Heisenberg demonstrated that the elements of all energy matter in the universe, out there or down here, consist of quanta of information. Light.

During the Roaring 20th Century, the equations of quantum physics led to the development of quantum appliances that allowed humans to receive, process, and transmit electronic images. Telephone, cinema, radio, television, computers, compact discs, fax machines; suddenly humans were creating digital realities that were accessed on living-room screens.

This universe of electronic signals, in which we now spend so much time, has been called Cyberia.

Just as the fish brain had to don dry-skin terra-suits to inhabit the Terrarium, and just as our primate brains had to don Canaveral space suits to explore outer space, our brains need cyberwear and digital appliances to inhabit cyberspace.

The Brain as a Digital Transmitter

As our brain evolves, it develops new vehicles and information-processing devices in order to feed its insatiable hunger for stimulation. Like any adolescent organ, the human brain requires an enormous, continual supply of chemical and electronic data to keep growing toward maturity.

In my last decade, the dendritic metabolism of my information organ—my brain—seems to have undergone a dramatic change. My eyes became two hungry mouths pressed against the Terrarium window through which electronic pulses reached the receptive areas of my brain. My brain seemed to require a daily input of several billion bytes of digital light speed information. In this I was no different from the average, televoid American sluggishly reclining on the bottom of the Terrarium. My brain also required regular diets of chemical foods. But my Very Personal Computer transformed my brain into an output organ emitting, discharging digital information through the Terrarium window into ScreenLand.

Just as my heart was programmed to pump blood, my sinewy brain was programmed to fire, launch, transmit, beam thoughts through the electronic window into Cyberia. The screen became the revolving glass door through which my brain both received and emited her signals.

As a result of personal computers and video arcades, millions of us are no longer satisfied to peer like passive infants through the Terrarium wall into the ScreenLand filled with cyber stars like Bill and Hillary and Boris and Obama and Paris Hilton and Beavis and Butt Head. We are learning how to enter and locomote in Cyberia. Our brains are learning how to exhale as well as inhale in the datasphere.

Of course, not all humans will make this move. Many of our finny ancestors preferred to remain marine forms. "You'll never get me up in one of those," said the tadpole to the frog.

Many humans will be trapped by gene-pool geography or compelled by repressive societies or seduced by material rewards and thus re-side in the material-flesh world of mammalian bipeds. Oh, yeah. To escape from the boredom and to rest alter their onerous, mech-flesh la-bors, they will torpidly ingest electronic realities oozing from their screens; but they will not don cyber suits and zoom into ScreenLand.

We tri-brains who learn to construct and in-habit auto-realities spend some time in the cyber world and some in the material-organic world. We zoom through the datmosphere like Donkey Kongs and Pac Woman, scooping up info-bits and spraying out electronic-reality forms. And then we cheerfully return to the slow, lascivious, fleshy material world to indulge our bodies with sensory stimulation and to exercise our muscles by pushing around mechanical realities in sport or recreation.

On the skin-tissue plane, our left brains are limited to mechanical-material forms. But in ScreenLand our right brains are free to imagi-neer digital dreams, visions, fic-tions, concoctions, hallucinatory adventures. All these screen scenes are as real as a kick-in-the-pants as far as our brains are concerned. Our brains have no sense organs and no muscles. Our brains command our bodies and send spaceships to the Moon by sending signals in only one linguistic: the quan-tum language of zeros and ones.

> **In ScreenLand our right brains are free to imagineer digital dreams, visions, fictions, concoctions, hallucinatory adventures.**

No More Mind-Body Paradox

 We tri-brain creatures seem to be resolving that most ancient philosophic problem. Forget the quaint, mammalian dualism of mind versus body. The interplay of life now involves digital brain-body matter-digital screen.

Everything—animal, vegetable, mineral, tangible, invisible, electric—is converted to digital food for the info-starved brain. And now, using the new digital appliances, everything that the brain mind can conceive can be realized in electronic patterns.

To be registered in consciousness, to be "realized," every sensory stimulation must be deconstructed, minimalized, digitalized. The brain converts every pressure signal from our skins, tickles from our genitals, delectables from our tongues, photons from our eyes, sound waves from our ears, and, best of all, electronic buzziness from our screens into quantum realities, into directories and files of 0/1 signals.

We tri-brain amphibians are learning how to use cyber wear—computer suits—to navigate around our ScreenLands the way we use the hardware of our bodies to navigate around the material-mechanical world, and the way we use spaceships and space suits to navigate around the outer space.

There are some amusing and alluring philosophic by-products. Quantum psychology allows us to define, operationally, other terms of classical metaphysics.

A Definition of "Spiritual" Could Be "Digital"

Recite to yourself some of the traditional attributes of the word "spiritual"—mythic, magical, ethereal, incorporeal, intangible, nonmaterial, disembodied, ideal, platonic. Is that not a definition of the electronic-digital?

Can We Engineer Our Souls?

Can we pilot our souls? The closest you are probably ever going to get to navigating your soul is when you are piloting your mind through your brain or its external simulation on cybernetic screens. Think of the screen as the cloud chamber on which you can track the vapor trail of your platonic, immaterial movements. If your digital footprints and spiritual fingerprints look less than soulful on the screen, well, just change them. Learning how to operate a soul figures to take time.

The quantum-electronic universe of information defines the new spiritual state. These "spiritual" realms, over centuries imagined, may, perhaps, now be realized! The more philosophic among us find this philosophically intoxicating.

Amphibians Will Not Neglect the Body

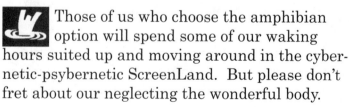 Those of us who choose the amphibian option will spend some of our waking hours suited up and moving around in the cybernetic-psybernetic ScreenLand. But please don't fret about our neglecting the wonderful body.

The first point to register is this: We tri-brains should not use our precious fleshware to work. Is it not a sacrilegious desecration to waste our precious sensory equipment on toil, chore, drudgery? We are not pack animals, or serfs, or executive robots garbed in uniforms rushing around lugging briefcases to offices. Why should we use our priceless, irreplaceable bodies to do work that can be done better by assembly-line machines?

But who will plough the fields and harvest the grapes? The languorous Midwestern farmer will done her cybersuit and while reclining in her hammock in Acapulco she will operate the automated plough on her Nebraska farm. The winemaker while reclining in his hammock on vacation in Acpulco will use his cybergear to direct the grape-crushing machines.

When we finish our work, we will take off our cybersuits, our brain clothing, and don body clothes. When we platonic migrants sweat, it will be in athletic or sensual pleasure. When we exert elbow grease, it will be in some form of painterly flourish or musical riff. When we operate oil gulping machines, we will joyride for pleasure. The only mechanical vehicles we will actually climb into and operate by hand will be sports cars. Trains, planes, boats will be used only for pleasure cruising, and will transport our bodies for athletic, artistic, recreational purposes only. Our bodily postures will thus be graceful and proud, our body movements delightful, slow, sensual, lush, erotic, fleshly, carnal vacations from the accelerated, jazzy cyber realities of cyberspace, where the brain work is done.

Personal Appearance in the Precious Flesh

Face-to-face interactions will be reserved for special, intimate, precious, sacramentalized events. Flesh encounters will be rare and thrilling. In the future each of us will be linked in thrilling cyber exchanges with many others whom we may never meet in person and who do not speak our phonetic literal language. Most of our important creations will take place in ScreenLand. Taking off our cyber wear to confront another with naked eyeballs will be a precious personal appearance. And the quality of our "personal appearances" will be raised to a level of mythic drama.

Common-Sense Quantum Psychology

 Before I acquired a personal computer, the principles of quantum physics always seemed, to my immature material mind, to be incomprehensible, bizarre, abstract, and totally impractical. After my digital brain lobes had been activated, quantum physics seems to make common sense and to define a practical psychology of everyday life in the tri-brain mode.

Einstein's theories of relativity, for example, suggest that realities depend on points of view. Instead of the static absolutes of space-time defined by material reality, quantum-brain realities are changing fields defined by quick feedback interchanges with other information sources. Our computer brainware allows us to perform Einsteinian-spiritual transformations on our laptops.

Werner Heisenberg's principle states that there is a limit to objective determinacy. If everyone has a singular viewpoint, constantly changing, then everyone creates his or her own version of reality. This gives the responsibility for reality construction not to a bad-natured biblical God, or to an impersonal, mechanical process of entropic devolution, or to an omniscient Marxist state, but to individual brains. Subjective determinacy operates in ScreenLand. Our brains create our own spiritual worlds, as they say along the Ganges. We get the realities we deserve. Or preserve. Or construct

And now our interactivated brains can project wonderland realities onto our screens and hurl them around the globe at light speed. Notice the political implications. Quantum psychology stressing singularity of viewpoint is the ultimate democratic perspective. The screen is the window to the new world. Who controls our screens programs the realities we inhabit. Therefore it behooves us to control our own reality screens.

These two notions, of relativity and self determination, are street smart common sense. But Einstein and Heisenberg and Max Planck and Niels Bohr lost the crowd when they said that the basic elements of the universe were bits of off/on yin/yang information. And that solid matter is temporary clusters of frozen information. And that when material structures are fissioned, they release energy: $E=mc^2$.

These brilliant physicists were explaining electronic

Learning how to operate a soul takes time.

The brain is an organ designed to metabolize digital information.

ideas by using their hands to write with paleolithic chalk on a slab of black slate!

During the next twenty to eighty years, quantum appliances became household items. The application of quantum physics to engineering produced vacuum tubes, transistors, integrated circuits, lasers, radio, television, computers. These gadgets are not intended to move "matter energy" around. Instead, they move information. Data-buzzes. Electronic means "informational." Sticks and stones may break your bones, but information can never hurt you. Although it can, alas, totally control your mind.

So it becomes clear that the basic "particles" that make up matter are bits of "information." Matter is frozen information. Energy is just the dumb smoke and sweat that matter releases in its lumbering transformations. The famous formula changes to: $I=mc^2$, where *"I"=information.*

At the quantum level the Newtonian "laws" turn out to be local ordinances. It turns out that the smaller the linguistic element, the greater the I.Q.—Information Quotient. The larger is always the lumbering vehicle for the miniaturized, platonic info units it carries around. The universe is an intelligence system, and the elements of intelligence are quanta. And suddenly we understand that the brain is an organ designed to metabolize digital information.

Quantum Psychology in the Roaring 20th Century

Except to those who had studied the brilliantly intuitive metaphors of oriental philosophy, these principles of quantum psychology sounded implausible and weird when they were first announced around A.D. 1900. But looking back we can see that every decade of the Roaring 20th Century has produced events that have confirmed and applied quantum principles.

The philosophy of the 20th century, since Peirce and Saussure, is linguistic, semiotic, semantic. So is the psychology, and the politics. Modern art, modern writing, modern music made us feel comfortable in the quantum atmosphere. The great artists dissolved representational structure, freed elements to create new forms, word patterns, sounds, and accepted the responsibility of subjective reality-formation. As Walk Disney demonstrated, the brain loves to be electronized.

And now we have interpersonal computers, power gloves, CDs and DVDs, IPODS, social networking sites, electronic bulletin boards. All of these place the power to create platonic, electronic realities in the hands of interacting individuals.

Exploring the Brain

The advent of psychedelic—mind-opening—drugs in the Sixties produced a widespread fascination with consciousness alteration, mind exploration, inner searching, brain-stimulation gadgets, oriental yoga—all based on quantum principles. The advent of personal and interpersonal computers, digital editors, and audio-video gear at the end of the century turned the average American home into an electronic-information center. At the same time, neurologists were publishing their discoveries about how neurotransmitter chemicals and electrical nets move information around the brain.

The convergence of these waves of information, the inner psychedelic and the ScreenLand cybernetic, made it possible for the first time for human beings to understand how the brain operates. The human brain is, by auto definition, the most powerful control communication unit in the known universe. A constellation of a hundred billion cells floating in an ocean of info-gel. The brain has no muscles and no sense organs. It is a shimmering sea swarming with microchip molecules packaged in enormous hardware neurons, all linked by chemical-electrical signals. We could not understand how the brain operates until our electrical engineers built computers. And now we are learning how to beam our brain waves into the Cyberia of electronic reality, to think and play and work and communicate and create at this basic 0/1 level.

> **Our hundred-billion-neuron bio-computer brains are designed to process digital signals at the rate of a hundred fifty million per second.**

Our hundred-billion-neuron computers are designed to process digital signals at the rate of a hundred fifty million per second. Each neuron can unfold as many as ten thousand dendrite receptors to pick up information from its neighbors. Talk about local-area networks! Talk about Central Intelligence Activity! More information is probably exchanged per second at the site of one synapse than in the CIA headquarters in a day. If any.

This is the reality field that Plato described in the 4th Century B.C., that quantum mechanics intuited in 1900, and that we tri-brains began to inhabit at the end of the Roaring 20th Century.

Power to the Singularities

The nature of the quantum politics of thought processing and the human-computer interaction was dramatically changed by the introduction and marketing of digital home appliances.

We can now create electronic realities on the other side of the screen not just with a keyboard or a joystick or a mouse. We wear the interface. We don cybergloves, cybergoggles, cybercaps, cybervests, cybershorts! Our bodily movements create the images on our screens. We walk, talk, dance, swim, float around in digital worlds, and we interact on screens with others who are linked in our nets.

Cyberwear is a mutational technology that allows individual's brains to experience OOB—out-of-body—experiences just as landware like legs and lungs permitted the fish to escape the water— OOW experiences. Cyberwear will make it possible for individual Americans to cross the Merlin Wall and to meet and interact in cyberspace.

Pioneers of Cyberspace

The basic notion of OOB artificial-reality appliances was introduced by Myron Kreuger and Ted
Nelson in the 1970s. The nitty-gritty realities of
creating and inhabiting digital universes were
described in 1985 by William Gibson in his brilliant, epic trilogy *Neuromancer Count Zero*, and
Mona Lisa Overdrive. Gibson described the "ma-
trix," the dataworlds created by human digital
communication. By 1989 cybernauts like Jaron
Lanier, Eric Gullichsen, Joi Ito, Brenda Laurel,
and Rebecca Allen were developing cyberspace
realities built for two. Or more.

Realities Built for Two

Many people are understandably disturbed by
the idea that in the future human beings will be
spending more time in ScreenLand than in Flesh
Play; piloting their brain-selves inside electronic
realities, interacting with other electronic humans.

Like adolescents whose hormones suddenly
awaken the unused sexual circuits of their brains,
we tri-brains are just now discovering that the brain
is an info-organ wired, fired, and inspired to process
and emit electronic signals. The main function of a
computer is interpersonal communication.

Soon many of us will be spending almost all our
screen time actively zooming around digital oceans
interacting and recreating with other tri-brains.

Some industrial-age cynics say that humans
are too lazy. They would rather sit back as sed-
entary couch slugs than be active. But we've
been through these tech-jumps before in history.

Before Henry Ford, only big shot engineers and captains employed by corporations drove mass-media vehicles such as trains and steamboats. Now we recognize—and often deplore—this genetic compulsion to grab the steering wheel, smoke rubber, and freely auto mobilize that sweeps over every member of our species at puberty.

Soon most of our daily operations—occupational, educational, recreational—will transpire in ScreenLands. Common sense suggests that we are more likely to find compatible brainmates if we are not restricted to local geography or to physical bodies.

Cyberwear will make it possible for individual Americans to cross the Merlin Wall and to meet and interact in cyberspace.

3

CUSTOM-SIZED SCREEN REALITIES

For thousands of years, since the dawn of tribal societies, most human beings have lived in drab caves, huts, shacks, igloos, houses, or apartments furnished and supplied with minimum information equipment-oral-body language. Stone tools.

In these shut-in, introverted, inward-looking, data-starved abodes occurred the practical maintenance time-dons that people had to perform to keep the gene pool going. For most people the plumbing was crude, the clothing hardly seductive. Cosmetics and perfumes were minimal—to say the most.

In the tribal culture there were no books, radios, or daily newspapers. No *Vogue* magazine loaded with five hundreds slick pages of silk fashion, voluptuous models pouting with desire, straining to arouse, flashing wide-open, inviting legs in high-heeled shoes, and curving, suck-me tits. No, the survival information needed to maintain the tribal home was packaged in rote, monkey-like signals expressed by the body: oral grunts, gestures, bodily movements, crude artifacts.

The Tribal-Culture Show

If we wanted to experience a bit of glamour, if we yearned to flirt around, looking for a sexual partner, or to check on what was happening, if we needed a battery recharge to keep us going as a loyal gene-pool serf-servant, we had to exit the home and amble up to the village square. There we could get the evening tribal news, pick up the local gossip, and make deals for skins or fur coats for our wives in exchange for a stone knife.

On designated occasions, our entire tribe would swarm together for ceremonies of celebration: Planting. Harvesting. Full moons. Solstice flings. Weddings. Funeral orgies. In agricultural societies the ingestion of psychotropic vegetables has always provided the sacramental energy for the gene-pool gatherings. Wines, fermented grains, brain change vines, roots, leaves, flowers containing the precious neurotransmitters prepared and administered by alchemical shamans produced the "high," the venerable, sacred, precious transcendental state of chaotics, ecstasy, possession, revelation, trance—the mythic-genetic right-brain vision. The Holy Confusion.

You know what I'm talking about. What orgasm is to the body, this shuddering psychedelic experience is to the brain.

At these treasured high moments, we tribe members could escape the drab and activate our individual myths, our special inner talents, and we could communicate it to others who were navigating their own personal neurorealities.

These intense communications, brain exchanges which Catholics call "Holy Communion," we call the Holy Confusion. At these ceremonies we tribe members could express our visions in communal theatre. This one becomes a jokester. Another sings. Another dances. Suddenly tricksters, artists, mimes take the center stage to act out the emotions and the identifying themes that held the tribe together.

Sponsors of the tribal show time?

The clique that ran the tribe. The priests and the chieftains. The lovable grey beards, the stern, traditional Old Ones. The studio heads. Those responsible for holding the tribe together for their own fame and profit

The task of luring the populace to listen to the sponsors' messages in the feudal-industrial ages was delegated to a special caste called: The talent. The painters. The directors. The shaman. The architects. The entertainers. The minstrels. The storytellers. Their function and duty in the tribal economy was to calm the fears of Chaos with delightful comforting fantasies, titillating ceremonies, and romantic dramas.

We could let our swollen, tumescent eyeballs pop wide open and our turgid, drooling peasant tongues dangle as we watched the belly dancers and muscular dudes wiggle, writhe, slither, jiggle, and quiver until our loins ached. When we were back in the

What orgasm is to the body, this shuddering psychedelic experience is to the brain.

dark cave/hut in fireplace flicker, our plain, glamourless, loyal mates suddenly turned into the Whores of Babylon! Krishnas with glowing hardons! Talk about pornography inciting desire!

The perennial problem with the directors and the talent is this. To attract and dazzle villagers to listen to the commercials, they had to allow the public to vicariously experience this steamy, smoking hot, exciting, naughty stuff that was absolutely taboo for the people, but which could be acted out in morality plays, racy festival performances, sculptures of naked bodies. And here's where we talents come in.

To keep the folks tuning in, the sponsors needed us performers. The sexy musicians, well-endowed dancers, clowns, raunchy comedians telling risque stories about adulteries and risky new sexual adventures, poets, X-rated storytellers, comics, mimes. It was the talent who performed the safety-valve function, who gave the populace a fantasy taste of the rich and forbidden fruits.

Talents were selected for beauty, erotic charm, powerful emotion. We were expected to go too far, to push the envelope of taboo, to test the limits of good taste. Show our tits and asses. Act out wild copulatory sex dances. Scandalize. And we were required to suffer the consequences. We were banned. Blacklisted. Sold down the river. Forced into harlotry. Fired from Harvard. Forever shamed and exposed in the local version of the perennial *National Enquirer*. Denounced as devils from the pulpits of the orthodox preachers, and denounced as C.I.A. agents by Marxists.

The sponsors of the tribal show, the priests and the chiefs, were kept busy not only producing the event, but also watching and censoring and punishing to make sure that nothing got too far out of hand, or upset the sponsors. And, of course, the gene-pools commercials were ever-present. We could never forget who owned the drums and the rattles and the spears and the shamanic talent, and the temples. The patrons who paid for the tribal show.

4

THANK GOD FOR FEUDALISM

Marshall McLuhan spoke wisely. "Change the media and you change the culture." Literacy upgraded the aesthetic level and the efficiency of the entertainment packaging. The growth of cities and nations by the 1st Century B.C. provided big budgets and big crews to distribute continual messages from the gene-pool sponsors.

The people, the average folk, the sixpack-Joe families, were now called plebes or serfs or peasants. Their role in the feudal-information economy was not that different from that of their tribal ancestors. The poor people are always seen as primitive because they are forced to live in tribal neighborhoods, ghettos, in huts, shacks, windowless rooms, slum pads, shabby urban caves where the signal rate was limited to immediate biological data exchanges from first breath to death.

The cultural and political messages from the sponsors of the feudal age were popularized and disseminated in spectacular public broad-

casts. The church in the central plaza was large,
ornate, decorative, loaded with statues and
paintings of truly inspired aesthetic genius. The
mediaeval crime time show, both Christian and
Islamic, was performed by miraculously gifted
talent. The tiled mysteries of the Alhambra and
the ceilings of the Vatican Chapel still inspire
the breathless reflex reaction, "Wow! Praise the
Lord for sponsoring this great show!"

Every day the commercial logos and mottoes
of the feudal culture were repeated. The muez-
zin's call, the church bell's sonorous clang, the
chanting of the monks, the colorful garb of the
priests and mullahs. Stained glass!

No wonder these feudal religions—fundamentalist, fanatic, furious, passionate, paranoid
—swept the Hooper ratings! The fellaheen could
leave their scruffy hovels and walk through
cathedrals with golden ceilings stretching to the
sky, while candles flickered on the statues of
the Prophet. A panoramic mosque-church scene
throbbing with color, pomp, grandeur, wealth,
and melodrama pouring into virginal eyeballs.

The palaces of the secular rulers, the kings
and dukes, were equally stunning, and much
more sexy. The priests may have preached sexual abstinence, but the nobles forked anyone they
wanted to and celebrated sexual beauty in the
paintings they commissioned. The walls of the
palaces glowed with flamboyant celebrations
of naked wantonness. Greek

The walls of the palaces glowed with flamboyant celebrations of naked wantonness.

goddesses with pink, swollen thighs and acres of soft, silky flesh sprawled on clouds of filmy desire, enticing their male counterparts to enjoy their favors.

You could stand humbly with cap in hand and cheer the swells dressed up in opulent lace and leather riding by in gold-decorated carriages. You loved the changing of the Guard, probably not realizing that the troops were there to protect the sponsors of the show from you, the people.

The shack you live in may be dreary, but ankle downtown to catch the big, spectacular God-King show.

Change the media

and you change the culture.

—*Marshall McLuhan*

5

THANK GUTENBERG-NEWTON FOR THE INDUSTRIAL AGE

The same McLuhan trends continued in the industrial age. As usual, the populace was housed in small, dark rooms, but now that big is better, the rooms were stacked in enormous slum buildings.

The factory culture created the highest form of intelligent life on this planet, up until now: the mass-market consumer.

The sponsors of the factory economy didn't really plan to create an insatiable consumer class that would eventually overwhelm it with acquisitive desire. Quite the contrary. The sponsors of the industrial culture were those who belonged to the one class that easily survived the fall of feudalism: the engineer-managers. They were sometimes called Masons. They were white, anti-papist, Northern European mechanics, efficient and rational, with a scary hive mentality totally loyal to The Order. Stem puritans. They worked so hard, postponed so much pleasure, and got obsessed with engineering so efficiently that they ended up flooding the world with an unstoppable cascade of highly appealing products. Labor saving devices. Better medicines to save lives. Better guns to snuff lives. Books. Radios. Televisions.

This cornucopian assembly line of everything that a tribal hunter or a feudal serf or a Holy Roman Emperor could possibly have lusted for required endless rotating armies of indefatigably industrious consumers willing to lift items from shelves, haul grocery carts, unpack bags, store in refrigerators, kick tires, read manuals of instruction, turn keys, drive away, and then religiously repair, until death, the appliances that rolled like an endless river of metal-rubber-plastic down Interstate 101 to the shopping malls and into our factory-made homes.

How can the sponsors keep the people motivated to perform the onerous tasks of producing and consuming at a feverish pace? The same old way—by putting on a show and promising them a glimpse of the high life. But this time, in the mercantile culture, they can sell 'em tickets.

The cultural celebrations that got people out of the house in the industrial society were no longer religious-political ceremonies. They occurred in commercial venues. Public invited. Tickets at box office or street corner. Every community boasted a theatre, concert hail, art gallery, opera house, burlesque pal-

The factory culture created the highest form of intelligent life on this planet, up until now: The Mass-Market Consumer.

ace, vaudeville show, sports stadium, bullring.
Etcetera. These entertainment factories were
built to resemble the royal structures of the feudal age. Theatres were called the "Palace" and
the "Majestic" and the "Royal."

In these plastic-fantastic whorehouse temples, workers could escape the routine, drab
signalry of the workday and lose themselves in
lascivious, wet-dream, hypnotic states of erotic
pleasure, tantalizing, carnal carnivals designed
and produced by us, the shamanic profession,
the counterculture entertainers.

The psycho-economics were clear-cut. The
consumers wanted the show to last as long as
possible, anything to get out of the hovel. More
was better. The show-biz trick was to stretch out
the scenes of the opera, stage play, concert as
long as possible. Give 'em their money's worth.

Films Present Electric Realities

 By the mid-20th Century, at the peak of
the mechanical age, the relentless engineering search for labor saving devices
and mass distribution naturally extended to the
entertainment industry. The new McLuhan media was electricity. Stage plays could be filmed,
the films duplicated and sent to hundreds of
theatres.

The effect was astounding. Farmer Brown
could sit in the village theatre and there in front
of him, thirty-feet high, was the face of Clara
Bow, her bulging red lips glistening with mois-
ture, her eyes beaming nymphomaniac invita-

tion! Farmer Brown had never in his wildest fantasies dreamed of this sultry thang! Meanwhile, Mrs. Brown is breathing Hard and leaking her precious bodily juices watching Rudolf Valentino licking his full lips with his sensual tongue

What Industrial Minds Want

Movies swept the world. The film industry naturally followed the commandment of the mechanical age—bigger is better. Cloned quantity is better. Feature films were made in two convenient sizes. The epic was very long. But the industry was run by clothing merchants from New York who knew how to sell, cut-rate, two pants to a suit. So most films were manufactured in the half size "double-bill." If and when the people left their homes and traveled downtown to the theatre, they expected a good three or four hours of escape.

Over the last twenty-five thousand years, until yesterday, the sponsors had come and gone, and the technologies had improved from oral-gestural to hand-tool to mechanical-electric. But the goals, principles, and venues of human motivation and human communication hadn't really changed much, and the economics hadn't changed. Big was always better.

The talent in tribal, feudal, and industrial cultures had two "charm" tasks. The first, and most important, was to entice, beg, grovel, seduce, use our sexual wiles, go down on our knees to the sponsors to get the deal. The second job was to please the customers. This was easier, because the customers basically were begging to get titillated, turned on, aroused. They had paid money to adore the talent.

The sponsors, of course, got their kicks from flicking over everyone, especially the glamorous talent. When and if the entertainers became superstars, they, naturally, got off their knees, wiped off their mouths, and proceeded to take exquisite revenge on the sleazy producers, the grubby studio heads, the rodent-like agency executives, the greedy managers, and the assorted lawyer thieves with briefcases and fax machines who had formerly abused us.

"There's no business like show business!" As they were fond of saying.

Learn How to Change the Screens

These ancient rituals, which endured through the tribal, feudal, industrial ages, amazingly enough, began to change dramatically in the last few years! Just before yesterday, around 1984, a combination of American creativity and Japanese precision suddenly mass-produced inexpensive, do-it-yourself home appliances for individuals to electronify, digitize, and transmit personal realities.

Digital communication translates the recording of any sound or photograph of any image into clusters of quanta or fuzzy clouds of off/on information. Any image digitized by an individual human can then be flashed on telephone lines around the world inexpensively at light speed.

Bigger is No Longer Better

The basic elements of the youniverse, according to quantum-digital physics, can be understood as consisting of quanta of information, bits of compressed digital programs, These elements of pure (0/1) information contain incredibly detailed algorithms to program potential sequences for fifteen billion years—and still running. These information-jammed units have only one hardware external function. All they do is flash off/on when the immediate environment triggers a complex array of "if if if if ... THEN!" algorithms.

Digital communication (i.e., the operation of the universe) involves massive arrays of these info units, trillions of information pixels flashing to create the momentary hardware reality of one single molecule.

The Newtonian energy- matter equations of the industrial age—the 19th Century—defined a local mechanical reality in which much bigger and more was very much better. You remember the catch-phrases in the old Newtonian heavy metal Dinosaur Marching Song? Force. Momentum. Mass. Energy. Work. Power. Thermodynamics.

In the information age when packaging digital data, much smaller is very much better.

In the information age we are coming to realize that in packaging digital data, much smaller is very much better.

The basic principle in light-speed communication is that so much more information is

packed into so much smaller hardware units.
For example, the 2-pound human brain is a digital organic computer that processes a hundred
million times more information (r.p.m.) than the
200-pound body.

The almost invisible DNA code keeps programming and constructing improved organic
computing appliances, i.e., generation after
generation of better and more portable brains. A
billion-year-old DNA megaprogram of invisible
molecular size is much smarter than the shud-
deringly fragile, here-and-now brain!

And infinitely smaller. People are learning
to deal with enormous stacks of digital-electronic information presented at light speeds.
Telephone. Radio. Television. Computers. Compact discs. At home. In their "head" quarters.
Electronic info is pulled down from the sky and
poured out of the portable stereophonic ghetto-
blaster perched on shoulder, jacked into ear-balls
as the body dances along the avenue. This "addiction" to electronic information has drastically
expanded the reception scope and lessened the
tar pit attention span of the 19th Century.

Cybernetic Brains Expect More Data In Less Time

Folks in the mechanical age may be content to sit drinking tea and reading the
London Times for two hours. But energetic smart
people navigating a postindustrial brain move
through an ocean of information, surfing data
waves breaking at light speed.

This appetite for digital data, more and
faster, can now be recognized as a species need.

The brain needs electrons and psychoactive chemicals like the body needs oxygen. Just as body nutritionists list our daily requirements for vitamins, so will our brain-psyberneticians soon be listing our daily requirements for various classes of digital information.

Soon pure information will be cheaper than water and electricity. The average American home will be equipped to access trillions of bits of information per minute. The credit-card-size interpersonal computer will be able to scoop up any page from the Library of Congress, sift through the entire film library of MGM, sort through all the episodes of "I Love Lucy," and slice out—if it pleases you—paragraphs from the original Aramaic Bible.

On a typical Saturday way back in 1990, Los Angeles residents with a competitive itch could exercise the option to flick on seven major-league baseball games, nine college football contests, the Olympic games, two horse-racing tracks, etc.

Soon even the poorest kid in the inner city will have a thumbnail-size chip—costing a dollar—with the storage and processing power of a billion transistors. He/she will also have an optic-fiber wall socket that will input a million times more signals than the current television set. Inexpensive virtual-reality suits and goggles will allow this youngster to interact with people all over the world in any environment he or she chooses to fabricate

As George Gilder says, "The cultural limitations of television, tolerable when there was no alternative, are unendurable in the face of the new computer technologies now on the horizon-technologies in which the U.S. leads the world."

The smart home, thus equipped with inexpensive digital appliances, becomes our private television film-sound studio that programs the digital universe we choose to inhabit, for as long as we want to inhabit it.

But is there not a danger of overload? The ability to scan and fish-net miniaturized, abridged, slippery bursts of essence aesthetic information from the salty oceans of signals flooding the home becomes a basic survival skill in the 21st Century. Our bored brains love "overload." They can process more than a hundred million signals a second.

Of course, this acceleration and compression of information has already become state of the art in television. The aim of crime-time network television is to get people to watch commercials. A 30-second slot during the Super Bowl broadcast costs more than a million dollars.

The advertising agencies were the first to pick up the handy knack of digital-miniaturization. They spurt dozens of erotic, shocking, eye-catching images into a half-minute info-slot convincing us that "the night belongs to Michelob." For that matter, we select our presidents and ruling bureaucrats on the basis of 30-second image clips, carefully edited by advertising experts.

Bigger is Not Better—Even in Movies

Slowly, reluctantly, the factory-based film industry is being forced to condense, speed up. Veteran, old -y are trapped in the antiquated industrial-age models of the opera and the "legitimate" stage play and the epic movie. And the prima-donna omnipotent director.

Before 1976, the bigger the movie the better. The long, leisurely, time-consuming film was the great epic. A director who came into the screening room with anything less than 2 hours—120 minutes or 7200 seconds—was considered a breezy lightweight.

Way back in 1966, before cable television, people loved long, slow films. They provided folks with a welcome escape from their info-impoverished homes. You went to the theatre to enter a world of technicoloured glamour and excitement that could not be experienced at convenience in the living room. In the theatre you could be Queen for a Night. The director, naturally enough, tried to stretch out the show as long as possible to postpone the customer's return to the home dimly lit by three black-and-white television networks.

This appetite for digital data, more and faster, can now be recognized as a species need.

Miniaturization

By the beginning of the century, however, most American residences were equipped with cable inputs and DVDs and remote controls, with flat

screen TV coming in fast. Sitting like sultans
in botanical torpor, we browse, graze, nibble
as many multitone, flashing screen-fix as our
warm little fingers can punch buttons.

We are no longer sensation-starved serfs
pining in dark garrets, lusting, longing, crav-
ing, starved for the technicolour flash of soft
curving flesh. On late night television we can
bathe in sexual innuendo. We can rent X-rated
films of every erotic version and perversion ever
dreamed. There is no longer that desperate appetite, that starved hunger, that yearning itch,
that raw hankering for optical stimulation.

For this reason the long, slow, symphony-
scored feature film has become a plodding line
of 150 elephants trapped in the melodramatic
swamp. Movies today are far too long. The
information-age cyber-person simply will not

**We are no longer
sensation-starved serfs.**

sit for 150 minutes trapped in Cimino's wonderfully operatic mind or Coppolla's epic intensi-
ties. For many of us, the best stuff we see on a
movie screen are the trailers. A new art form is
emerging—the production of 3-minute teasers
about coming attractions. Electronic haikus!
Most movies fail to live up to the trailers that
hype them. The "high lights" of a smash-grab
action flick can be fascinating for 3 minutes,
but lethally boring for 2 hours. Indeed, most of
the new breed of movie directors learned their
craft by making commercials or MTV clips,
from which have come the new communication
rhythms.

The brain needs electrons and psychoactive chemicals like the body needs oxygen. Just as body nutritionists list our daily requirements for vitamins, so will our brain-psyberneticians soon be listing our daily requirements for various classes of digital information.

Filmmakers are learning the lesson of quantum physics and digital neurology: much more data in much smaller packages. It turns out that the brain likes to have digital signals jamming the synapses.

Custom-Sized Movies

In response to this obvious fact, some innovative filmmakers are beginning to experiment with customized movies, sized for length. The idea is this. If you go to a good restaurant, you don't want to sit trapped at a table for 150 minutes eating the same Italian dish. No matter how delicious. No matter how many Oscars the chef has won, most younger film buffs are not gonna sit still during a 2 1/2-hour spaghetti film by moody, self-absorbed auteur-directors from the operatic traditions.

But if long, slow flicks are what you want, if you really prefer to absorb electronic information like a python ingests a pig, if you want to stuff yourself and slowly digest a 150-minute film—why, no problem! You arrive at the cineplex and you make your menu selection when you buy your ticket. If you want the super-giant 150-minute version of *Last Temptation of Christ* you pay $20, visit the rest room, pack a lunch, cancel a few meetings, walk to the long-distance room, settle in, and let Scorcese leisurely paddle you down his cerebral canals. As a television person, your

> **The brain likes to have digital signals jamming the synapses.**

attention appetite at the visual banquet table probably gets satiated after an hour. So you'll tend to select the regular-size epic: Christ, $10 for 50 minutes.

But cyberplots and brain jocks, with an eternity of digitized info-worlds at fingertip, tend to go for the nouvelle cuisine, gourmet buffet. You pay $5 and watch five 10-minute "best-of," haiku compressions of five films. Five "high lights" essence-teasers. Tastes great! Less filling!

If you are really taken by one of these *specialite de maison* and want more, you either go to the box office for a ticket or you stick your credit card in the dispenser cabinet, dial your choice, and out pops a custom sized rental video to take home and scan at your convenience.

Do-It-Yourself Cyberware Offers Personal Electronic Realities

So far you have been a busy consumer with many passive selective options. But suppose you want to move into the active mode? Change the film? Script and direct your own version? Put your personal spin on the great director's viewpoint. Heresy!

Suppose, for example, that you're a 14-year-old African or Asian girl and you dislike the movie *Rambo*, which cost $40 million, minimum to make. You rent the video for $2 and scan it. Then you select the most offensive section. Maybe the one where Sly Stallone comes crashing through the jungle into the native village, naked to the waist, brandishing a machine gun with which he kills several hundred Asian men, women and children.

To present your version, you digitize this 30-second scene, copy it into your $100 Nin-Sega-Mac computer, and use the Director software program to re-edit. You digitize the torso of a stupid-looking gorilla, you can a wilted celery stalk or the limp penis of an elephant, you loop in the voice of Minnie Mouse in the helium mode screaming the Stallone lines: "You gonna let us win this time?"

You pass your version into the rented tape, pop it back in the box and return it to the video store. The next person renting *Rambo* will be in for a laugh and a half! Within weeks this sort of viral contagion of individual choice could sweep your town.

In the cybernetic age now dawning, "Digital Power to the People" provides everyone this inexpensive option to cast, script, direct, produce, and distribute his or her own movie. Custom-made, tallorized, in the convenient sizes—mammoth, giant, regular, and byte-sized mini.

Energetic smart people navigating a postindustrial brain move through an ocean of information, surfing data waves breaking at light speed.

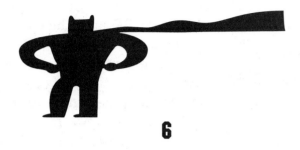

6

IMAGINEERING

I **remember viewing a videotape** filmed by cyberspace researchers at Autodesk, a Sausalito computer-software company. On the screen, a woman wearing tennis shorts leans ahead expecting a serve. On her head she wears a cap woven with thin wires. Her eyes are covered by opaque goggles. In her hand she holds a metal tennis racquet with no strings.

She dashes to her left and swings furiously at the empty air. "Oh no!" she groans in disappointment. "Too low!"

She crouches again in readiness then runs forward, leaps up, slams a vicious volley at the empty air and shouts in triumph.

The videotape then changes point of view. Now I am seeing what the player sees. I am in the court. The ball hits the wall and bounces back to my left. My racquet smashes the ball in a low-angle winning shot.

This woman is playing virtual racquet ball. Her goggles are two small computer screens

Does this sound too Star Trekky to be for real? Well, it's already happening.

showing the digitized three-dimensional picture of a racquetball court. She is in the court. As she moves her head-left, right, up-orientation-direction sensors in her cap show her the left wall, the right wall, the ceiling. The movement of the ball is calculated to reflect "real-life" gravity and spin.

I am experiencing the current big trend in electronics. It is called artificial reality or virtual reality or electronic reality. Some literary computer folks call it platonic reality, in honor of the Socratic philosopher who described a universe of idealized or imagined forms more than two thousand years ago. Cynics call it virtual banality.

We no longer need to press our addicted optical nostrils to the television screen like grateful amoebas. Now, we can don cybersuits, clip on cybergoggles, and move around in the electronic reality on the other side of the screen. Working, playing, creating, exploring with basic particles of reality-electrons.

This technology was first developed by NASA. The idea was that technicians in Houston could use their gloves to direct robots on the moon. Architects and engineers are experimenting with an Autodesk device to walk around in the electronic projections of the buildings they are designing. Doctors can travel down arteries and veins, observing and manipulating instruments.

Does this sound too Star Trekky to be for real? Well, it's already happening. Way back at Christmas 1990 six hundred thousand American kids equipped with Nintendo power gloves were sticking their hands through the Alice Window moving ninja warriors around.

The implications of this electronic technology for work and leisure and interpersonal intimacy are staggering.

For example, within a few years many of us will not have to "go" to work. We will get up in the morning, shower, dress in our cyberwear suits, and "beam" our brains to work. No more will we have to fight traffic in our air-polluting 300-horsepower cars, hunt for parking spaces, take the elevator to our offices. No more flying, strapped in our seats in a monstrous toxic-waste-producing air-polluting jet-propelled sky-dinosaur, jammed with sneezing, coughing sardines, fighting jet lag to attend conferences and meetings.

Tomorrow Our Brains Will Soar

Tomorrow our brains will soar on the wings of electrons into the offices of friends in Tokyo, then beam at light speed to a restaurant in Paris for a flirtatious lunch, pay a quick, ten-minute visit to our folks in Seattle—all without physically leaving our living rooms. In three hours of electronic, global house calls we can accomplish what would have taken three days or three weeks of lugging our brain-carrying bodies like slabs of inert flesh.

This is the information age, and the genera-tor-producers of information are our delightful, surprise-packed brains. Just as the enormously powerful machines of the industrial age moved our bodies around, so, tomor-row, will our cybernetic appliances zoom our brains around the world at light speed.

We will get up in the morning, shower, dress in our cyberwear suits, and "beam" our brains to work.

We won't travel to play. We press two buttons and we are standing on the tee of the first hole at Pebble Beach. There to join us is sister Anita—who is actually standing on the lawn of her house in Atlanta—and our dear-est, funniest, wonderful friend Joi, whom we have never met in the flesh—and who is actually standing in his backyard in Osaka. Each of us in turn "hits" the platonic golf ball and we watch them soar down the fairway. After finishing the first hole, we can dial-beam to Anita's patio to admire her garden, zap over to the tee of the second hole at St. Andrew's, then zoom to the Louvre to look at that Cezanne painting Joi was talking about.

Most of us Americans spend half our wak-ing hours zapping around in electronic environ-ments with our friends. Any spot in the world we can think of can be dialed up on our screens with our friends. Any landscape, surrounding, setting, habitat we can think of or imagine can be quick-ly fabricated on our screens with our friends.

Some thoughtful critics are concerned by the prospect of human beings spending so much time trapped like zombies in the inorganic, plastic-fantastic electronic world. They fear that this will lead to a depersonalization, a dehumanization, a robotization of human nature, a race of screen-addicted nerds. This understandable apprehension is grounded in the horrid fact that today the average American spends around six hours each day passively reclining in front of the boob tube, and three hours a day peering docilely into Big Brother's computer screens.

The optimistic human scenario for the future involves three common-sense steps.

1. Cure the current apathetic, torpid television addiction.

2. End the monopoly of top-down, spud-farm, mass-media centralized television, and

3. Empower individuals to actively communicate, perform, create electronic realities.

How? By means of inexpensive computer clothing.

Another example? A married couple, Tom and Jane, are walking down the Malibu beach. In material form, you understand. Real foot-massaging sand. Real skin-tanning sunshine blue sky. On loving impulse, they decide to spend a funny, loving minute or two with their daughter, Annie, who is in Boulder.

They flip down their lens-goggles that look like sunglasses. Jane punches a few numbers her stylish, designer wristwatch. Tom turns on the one pound Walkman receiver transmitter, In Boulder, Annie accepts their "visit" and dials them to a prefabricated pix scene of her patio. She is smiling in welcome. She is actually in her living room, but electrically she is in her electronic patio. They see exactly what they would see if they were there. When they turn their heads, they see Annie's husband Joe walking out waving. He points out the roses I have just bloomed in the garden. Remember, at the same time Tom and Jane are "really" walking down the Malibu beach. They can look over the goggles and watch two kids in bathing suits chasing a dog.

Reality designing is a team sport.

The four people sharing the "patio" reality decide they want to be joined by sister Sue, in Toronto. They dial her and she beams over to the "patio" in Colorado. Sue wants to show them her new dress; so the gang beams up to Sue's living room.

What'll It Cost?

It is logical for you, at this point, to wonder about the cost of transcontinental home movie-making. Is this not another expensive toy for affluent yuppies playing while the rest of the world starves?

Happily, the answer is "no." The equipment used by this family costs less than a standard television set, that pathetic junk-food spud-box with no power to store or process electronic information. Designing and digitizing and communicating the electronic realities costs less than a phone call. In ten years fiber-optic wires will receive transmit more information than all the clumsy air-wave broadcasting networks. A thumbnail size brain chip holding a billion transistors will allow us to store and process millions of three dimensional signals per minute. Intense chaotics waiting to be re-created.

What will we possibly do with these inexpensive extensions of our brains? The answer is so down to earth human. We shall use these wizard powers to communicate with each other at unimaginable levels of clarity, richness, and intimacy. Reality designing is a team sport.

Consider Erotic Interaction

To help us imagine one dimension of the communication possibilities, let us consider the erotic interaction. Cyril Connolly once wrote, "Complete physical union between two people is the rarest sensation which life can provide—and yet not quite real, for it stops when the telephone rings."

Connolly's comment is useful because he distinguishes between "physical" communication, bodies rubbing, and neurological signals—words and thoughts transmitted electrically. The solution to his problem is simple. Electronic appliances are beautifully cooperative. (Hey, Cyril, if you don't want to be disturbed, just turn the gadget off when you head for the sack, and then turn it back on when you wish to.)

But let us examine a more profound implication. Connolly refers to "complete physical union" as "the rarest sensation which life can provide." Is he thereby denigrating the "union of minds and brains"? The interplay of empathy, wit, fantasy, dream, whimsy, imagination? Is he scorning "platonic love"? Is he implying that sex should be mindless genital acrobatics? A grim, single-minded coupling that can be disturbed by the platonic rapture of metaphysical sex? Or a phone call?

Here is a typical episode of erotic play that could happen the day after tomorrow. The two lovers, Terry and Jerry, are performing bodily intercourse beautifully with elegance and sensual skill, etc. They are also wearing platonic lenses. At one point Jerry touches her/his watch, and suddenly they are bodysurfing twelve-foot rainbow waves that are timed to their physical erotic moves. Sounds of liquid magnificence flood their ears. Terry giggles and touches her/his watch, and the waves spiral into a tunnel vortex down which they spin and tumble. They intercreate reality dances. Terry is a seething volcano over whom Jerry soars as a fearless eagle, while birds sing and the Earth stiffly breathes.

Plato was magnificently on beam when he said that the material, physical expressions are pale, crude distortions of the idea forms that are fabricated by the mind, the brain, the "soul."

Plato, it turns out, was magnificently on beam. He said that the material, physical expressions are pale, crude distortions of the idea forms that are fabricated by the mind, the brain, the "soul." We are talking about learning how to operate our minds, our brains, our souls. And learning the rudiments of mind-fucking, silky body juicy fucking, and brain-soul fucking.

In fact, most physical sex, even the most "complete unions", is no more than graceful motions unless enriched by brain fucking imagination. And here is the charming enigma, the paradoxical truth that dares not show its face. Usually, even in the deepest fusions, neither partner really knows what is flashing through that delightful, adorable mind of the other.

In the future the wearing of cyberclothing will be as conventional as the wearing of body-covering clothing. To appear with out your platonic gear would be like showing up in public stark naked. A new global language of virtual-signals, icons, 3-D pixels will be the lingua franca of our species, Instead of using words, we shall communicate in self-edited movie clips selected from

We are talking about learning how to operate our minds, our brains, our souls.

the chaotic jungles of images stored on our wrists.

The local vocal dialects will remain, of course, for intimate communication. Nothing from our rich, glorious past will be eliminated. When we extend our minds and empower our brains, we shall not abandon our bodies, nor our machines, nor our tender, secret love whispers.

We will drive cars, as we now ride horses, for pleasure. We will develop exquisite bodily expressions, not to work like efficient robots, but to perform acts of grace.

The main function of the human being in the 21st Century is "imagineering" and electronic-reality fabrication; to learn how to express, communicate, and share the wonders of our brains with others.

7

ARTIFICIAL INTELLIGENCE

In the Sixties, Hermann Hesse was revered by college students and art rowdies as the voice of the decade. He was a mega-sage, bigger than Tolken or Salinger, McLuhan or Bucky Fuller. Hesse's mystical, utopian novels were read by millions. The popular, electrically amplified rock band Steppenwolf named themselves after Hesse's psyberdelic hero, Harry Halter, who smoked those "long, thin yellow immeasurably enlivening and delightful" cigarettes, then zoomed around the Theatre of the Mind, ostensibly going where no fictional heroes had been before.

The movie *Steppenwolf* was financed by Peter Sprague, at that time the Egg King of Iran. I lost the male lead to Max Van Sydow. Rosemary's part was played by Dominique Sanda. But that story is filed in another database.

Hesse's picaresque adventure, *The Journey to the East,* was a biggie too. It inspired armies of pilgrims—yours truly included—to hip-hike somewhere East of Suez, along the Hashish Trail to India. The goal of this Childlike Crusade? Enlightenment 101, an elective course.

Yes, it was that season for trendy Sufi mysticism, inner Hindu voyaging, breathless Buddhist searches for ultimate meaning. Poor Hesse, he seems out of place up here in the high tech, cybercool, Sharp catalogue, M.B.A., upwardly mobile 21st Century..

But our patronizing pity for the washed up Swiss sage may be premature. In the avant garde frontiers of the computer culture, around Massachusetts Avenue in Cambridge, around Palo Alto, in the Carnegie-Mellon AI labs, in the back rooms of the computer-graphics labs in Southern California, a Hesse comeback seems to be happening. This revival, however, is not connected with Hermann's mystical, eastern writings. It's based on his last, and least-understood work, Magister Ludi, or *The Glass Bead Game*.

This book, which earned Hesse the expense-paid brain ride to Stockholm, is positioned a few centuries in the future, when human intelligence is enhance and human culture elevated by a device for thought-processing called the glass-bead game.

Up here in the Electronic 2000s we can appreciate what Hesse did at the very pinnacle— Thirties and early Forties—of the smoke-stack mechanical age. He forecast with astonishing accuracy a certain postindustrial device for converting thoughts to digital elements and processing them. No doubt about it, the sage of the hippies was anticipating an electronic mind-appliance that would not appear on the consumer market until the mid-Seventies. I refer, of course, to the Fruit from the Tree of Knowledge called the Apple computer.

The Aldous Huxley-Hermann Hesse Fugue

I first heard of Hermann Hesse from Aldous
Huxley. He was reading Hesse and talked a lot
about his theory of human development. Huxley
was Carnegie Visiting Professor at MIT. His assignment: to give a series of seven lectures on the
subject, "What a Piece of Work Is Man." A couple
thousand people attended each lecture. Aldous
spent most of his off-duty hours hanging around
the Harvard Psychedelic Drug Research project
coaching us beginners in the history of mysticism
and the ceremonial care and handling of LSD,
which he sometimes called "gratuitous grace."

Hermann Hesse's
Three Stages of Human Development.

1. The tribal sense of tropical-blissful unity,

2. The horrid polarities of the feudal industrial societies, good evil, male female, Chris-
   tian-Moslem, etc., and

3. The revelatory rediscovery of The Oneness
   of It All.

No question about it, Hegel's three authoritarian thumbprints—thesis-antithesis-synthesis—
were smudged all over the construct, but Hesse
and Huxley didn't seem to worry about it, so why
should we untutored Harvard psychologists?

We all dutifully set to work reading Hesse.
Huxley claimed that his own spiritual intellectual development in England followed the devel-

opmental lifeline of Hesse in Germany. Aldous
delighted in weaving together themes from his
life that paralleled Hesse's.

Parodies of Paradise

Huxley's last book, *Island*, presents an atypi-
cal, tropical utopia in which meditation, gestalt
therapy, and psychedelic ceremonies create a
society of Buddhist serenity.

I spent the afternoon of November 20, 1963,
at Huxley's bedside, listening carefully as the dying philosopher spoke in a soft voice about many
things. He fashioned a pleasant little literary
fugue as he talked about three books he called
"parodies of paradise": his own *Island*, Orwell's
1984, and Hesse's *The Glass Bead Game*.

Aldous told me with a gentle chuckle that Big
Brother, the beloved dictator of Orwell's nightmare society, was based on Winston Churchill.
"Remember Big Brother's spell-binding rhetoric
about the blood, sweat, and fears requisitioned
from everyone to defeat Eurasia? The hate sessions? Priceless satire. And the hero's name is
Winston Smith,"

Aldous was, at that moment in time, fascinated by the *Tibetan Book of the Dying,* which I
had just translated from Victorian English into
American. The manuscript, which was later published as *The Psychedelic Experience,* was used by
Laura Huxley to guide Aldous' psychedelic passing.

Huxley spoke wryly of the dismal conclusions
of *Island, The Glass Bead Game*, and Orwell's
classic. His own idealistic island society was

crushed by industrial powers seeking oil. Hesse's utopian Castalia was doomed because it was out of touch with human realities. Then the crushing of love by the power structure in 1984. Unhappy endings. I timidly asked him if he was passing on a warning or an exhortation to me. He smiled enigmatically.

Two days later Aldous Huxley died. His passing went almost unnoticed, because John F. Kennedy also died on November 22, 1963. It was a bad day for utopians and futurists all over.

Ontological Evolution of Hermann Hesse

Hermann Hesse was born in 1877 in the little Swabian town of Caiw, Germany, the son of Protestant missionaries. His home background and education, like Huxley's, were intellectual, classical, idealistic. His life exemplified change and metamorphosis. If we accept Theodore Ziolkowski's academic perception, "Hesse's literary career parallels the development of modern literature from a fin de siècle aestheticism through expressionism to a contemporary sense of human commitment."

Voice of Romantic Escapism

Hesse's first successful novel, *Peter Camenzind*—published in 1904—reflected the frivolous sentimentality of the Gay Nineties, which, like the Roaring Twenties, offered a last fun frolic to a class society about to collapse.

"From aestheticism he shifted to melancholy realism. Hesse's novels fictionalize the admonitions of an outsider who urges us to question accepted values, to rebel against the system, to challenge conventional 'reality' in the light of higher ideals" (Ziolkowski).

Hesse made the obligatory mystical pilgrimage to India in 1911, and there, along the Ganges, picked up the microorganisms that were later to appear in a full-blown Allen Ginsbergsonian mysticism.

In 1914 Europe convulsed with nationalism and military frenzy. Hesse, like Dr. Benjamin Spock in another time warp, became an outspoken pacifist and war resister. Two months after the "outbreak of hostilities," he published an essay titled "0 Freunde, nicht dieser Tone" ["Oh Friends, Not These Tones"]. It was an appeal to the youth of Germany, deploring the stampede to disaster.

His dissenting brought him official censure and newspaper attacks. From this time on, Hesse was apparently immune to the ravages of patriotism, nationalism, and respect for authority.

Father of New-Age Psychology

Hesse's *Siddhartha* is the story of a Kerouac-Snyder manhood spent "on the road to Benares" performing feats of detached, amused, sexy one-upmanship.

In the June 1986 issue of *Playboy,* the Islamic yogic master and basketball superstar Kareen Abdul-Jabbar ("noble and powerful servant of Allah") summarized with his legendary cool the life stages he had experienced, using bead-

> **Hesse was apparently immune to the ravages of patriotism, nationalism, and respect for authority.**

game fugue techniques to weave together the
strand of his biography: basketball, racism, religion, drugs, sex, jazz, politics. "In my senior year
in high school," Abdul-Jabbar, "I started reading
everything I could get my hands on—Hindu texts,
Upanishads, Zen, Hermann Hesse—you name it!

Playboy: *"What most impressed you?"*

Abdul-Jabbar: *"Hesse's Siddhartha. I was
then going through the same things
that Siddhartha went through in his
adolescence, and I identified with his
rebellion against established precepts
of love and life. Siddhartha becomes an
aesthetic man, a wealthy man, a sensu-
ous man—he explores all these different
worlds and doesn't find enlightenment
in any of them. That was the book's
great message to me; so I started to develop my own value system as to what
was good and what wasn't."*

Steppenwolf, observes Ziolkowski, was greeted
as a "psychedelic orgy of sex, drugs, and jazz."
Other observers with a more historic perspec-
tive—present company included—have seen
Steppenwolf as a final send up of the solemn
polarities of the industrial age. Hesse mocks the
Freudian conflicts, Nietzschean torments, the
Jungian polarities, the Hegelian machineries of
European civilization.

Harry Hailer enters "The Magic Theatre.
Price of Admission: Your Mind." First he engages
in a "Great Automobile Hunt," a not too subtle
rejection of the sacred symbol of the industrial
age. Behind the door marked "Guidance in the

Building-Up of the Personality. Success Guaranteed!" H. H. learns to play a post-Freudian video game in which the pixels are part of the personality. "We can demonstrate to anyone whose soul has fallen to pieces that he can rearrange these pieces of a previous self *in what order he pleases* and so attain to an endless multiplicity of moves in the game of life."

This last sentence precisely states the basis for the many postindustrial religions of self-actualization. You learn how to put together the elements of your self in what order pleases you! Then press the advance key to continue.

The mid-life crisis of the Steppenwolf, his overheated Salinger inner conflicts, his Woody Allen despairs, his unsatisfied Norman Mailer longings, are dissolved in a whirling kaleidoscope of quick flashing neurorealities. "I knew," gasps H. H., "that all the hundred pieces of life's game were in my pocket.... One day I would be a better hand at the game."

The Glass-Bead Game Converts Thoughts to Elements

What do you do after you've reduced the heavy, massive boulder-like thoughts of your mechanical culture to elements? If you're a student of physics or chemistry you rearrange the fissioned bits and pieces into new combinations. Synthetic chemistry of the mind. Hesse was hanging out in Basel, home of Paracelsus. Alchemy 101. Solve et coagule. Recompose them in new combinations. You become a master of the bead game. Let the random-number generator shuffle your thought-deck and deal out some new hands!

Understandably, Hesse never gives a detailed description of this preelectronic data-processing appliance called the bead game. But he does explain its function. Players learned how to convert decimal numbers, musical notes, words, thoughts, images into elements, glass beads that could be strung in endless abacus combinations and rhythmic-fugue sequences to create a higher level language of clarity, purity, and ultimate complexity.

Global Language Based on Digital Units

Hesse described the game as "a serial arrangement, an ordering, grouping, and interfacing of concentrated concepts from many fields of thought and aesthetics."

In time, wrote Hesse, "the Game of games had developed into a kind of universal language through which the players could express values and set these in relation to one another."

In the beginning the game was designed, constructed, and continually updated by a guild of mathematicians called Castalia. Later generations of hackers used the game for educational, intellectual, and aesthetic purposes. Eventually the game became a global science of mind, an indispensable method for clarifying thoughts and communicating them precisely.

Evolution of the Computer

Hesse, of course, was not the first to anticipate digital thought processing. Around 600 B.C. the Greek Pythagoras (music of the spheres) and the Chinese Lao (yin yang)-tzu were speculating that all reality and knowledge could and should be expressed in the play of binary numbers. In 1832 a young Englishman, George Boole, developed an algebra of symbolic logic. In the next decade Charles Babbage and Ada Countess Lovelace worked on the analytic thought-engine. A century later, exactly when Hesse was constructing his "game" in Switzerland, the brilliant English logician Alan Turing was writing about machines that could simulate thinking, AI—artificial intelligence.

Hesse's unique contribution, however, was not technical, but social. Forty-five years before Toffler and Naisbitt, Hesse predicted the emergence of an information culture. In *The Glass Bead Game* Hesse presents a sociology of computing. With the rich detail of a World-Cup novelist (he won the Nobel Prize for Literature with this book) he describes the emergence of a utopian subculture centered around the use of digital mind-appliances.

Hesse understood that a language based on mathematical elements need not be cold, impersonal, rote.

Hesse then employs his favorite appliance, parody (cyber farce), to raise the disturbing question of the class division between the computer hip and the computer illiterate. The electronic elite versus the rag-and-glue proles with their hand-operated Coronas. The dangers of a two-tier society of the information rich and the information have-nots.

Forty-five years before Toffler and Naisbitt, Hesse predicted the emergence of an information culture.

Glorification of the Castalian Hacker Culture

The Glass Bead Game is the story of Joseph Knecht, whom we meet as a brilliant grammar-school student about to be accepted into the Castalian brotherhood and educated in the intricacies of the authorized thought-processing system. The descriptions of Castalia are charmingly pedantic. The reverent reader is awed by the sublime beauty of the system and the monk-like dedication of the adepts.

The scholarly narrator explains:

> *This Game of games . . . has developed into a kind of universal speech, through the medium of which the players are able to express values in lucid symbols and to place them in relation to each other.... A game can originate, for example, from a given astronomical configuration, a theme from a Bach fugue, a phrase of Leibnitz or from the Upanishads, and the fundamental idea awakened can be built up and enriched through assonances to relative concepts. While a moderate beginner can, through these symbols, formulate parallels between a piece of classical music and the formula of a natural law, the adept and Master of the Game can lead the opening theme into the freedom of boundless combinations.*

In this last sentence, Hesse describes the theory of digital computing. The wizard programmer can convert any idea, thought, or number into binary number chains that can be sorted into all kinds of combinations. We reencounter here the age long dream of philosophers, visionary poets, and linguists of a *universitas*, a synthesis of all knowledge, the ultimate data base of ideas, a global language of mathematical precision.

Hesse understood that a language based on mathematical elements need not be cold, impersonal, rote. Reading *The Glass Bead Game* we share the enthusiasm of today's hacker-visionaries who know that painting, composing, writing, designing, innovating with clusters of electrons (beads?) offers much more creative freedom than expressions limited to print on paper, chemical paints smeared on canvas, or acoustic (i.e., mechanical-unchangeable) sounds.

Hesse's Golden Age of Mind

In the Golden Age of Chemistry scholar-scientists learned how to dissolve molecules and to recombine the freed elements into endless new structures. Indeed, only by precise manipulation of the play of interacting elements could chemists fabricate the marvels that have so changed our world.

In the Golden Age of Physics, physicists, both theoretical and experimental, learned how to fission atoms arid to recombine the freed particles into new elemental structures. In *The Glass Bead Game* Hesse portrays a Golden Age of Mind. The knowledge information programmers of Castalla, like chemists and physicists, dissolve thought molecules into elements (heads) and weave them into new patterns.

In his poem, *The Last Glass Bead Game,* Hesse's hero Joseph Knecht writes, "We draw upon the iconography ... that sings like crystal constellations."

Technology Invents Ideology

Hesse apparently anticipated McLuhan's First Law of Communication: The medium is the message. The technology you use to package, store, communicate your thoughts defines the limits of your thinking. Your choice of thought tool determines the limitations of your thinking. If your thought technology is words-carved-into-marble, let's face it, you're not going to be a light-hearted flexible thinker. An oil painting or a wrinkled papyrus in a Damascus library cannot communicate the meaning of a moving-picture film. New thought technology creates new ideas. The printing press created national languages, the national state, literacy, the industrial age. Television, like it or not, has produced a global thought processing very different from oral and literate cultures.

Understanding the power of technology, Hesse tells us that the new mind culture of Castalla was based on a tangible mental device, a thought machine, "a frame modeled on a child's abacus, a frame with several dozen wires on which could be strung glass beads of various sizes, shapes, and colours."

Please do not be faked out by the toy-like simplicity of this device. Hesse has changed the units of meaning, the vocabulary of thought. This is serious stuff. Once you have defined the units of thought in terms of mathematical elements you've introduced a major mutation in the intelligence of your culture.

The Evolution of the Game

 The glass-bead appliance was first used by musicians: "The wires corresponded to the lines of the musical staff, the beads to the time values of the notes."

A bare two or three decades later the game was taken over by mathematicians. For a long while indeed, a characteristic feature of the game's history was that it was constantly preferred, used, and further elaborated by whatever branch of learning happened to be experiencing a period of high development or a renaissance.

At various times the game was taken up and imitated by nearly all the scientific and scholarly disciplines. The analytic study of musical values had led to the reduction of musical events to physical and mathematical formulae. Soon afterward, philology borrowed this method and began to measure linguistic configurations as physics measures processes in nature. The visual arts soon followed suit. Each discipline that seized upon the game created its own language of formulae, abbreviations, and possible combinations.

It would lead us too far afield to attempt to describe in detail how the world of mind, after its purification, won a place for itself in the state. Supervision of the things of the mind among the people and in government came to be consigned more and more to the intellectuals. This was especially the case with the educational system.

Artificial Intelligence & Alienated Hackers

"The mathematicians brought the game to a high degree of flexibility and capacity for sublimation, so that it began to acquire something of a consciousness of itself and its possibilities".

In this last phrase, Hesse premonitors Arthur C. Clarke and Stanley Kubrick's nightmare about neurotic artificial intelligence:

Dave: *"Open the pod doors, HAL."*

HAL: *"Sorry about that, Dave. This mission is too important to be threatened by human error."*

Hesse tells us that the first generations of computer adepts created a "hacker culture," an elite sect of knowledge processors who lived within the constructions of their own minds, disdaining the outside society. Then Hesse, with uncanny insight, describes the emergence of a phenomenon that has now become the fad in the information sciences.

The Artificial-Intelligence Cult

By 1984, billions of dollars were being spent in Japan (the so-called Fifth Generation projects), in America, and in Europe to develop artificial-intelligence programs. Those nations that already suffer from a serious intelligence deficit—Soviet Eurasia and the third-world nations—seem to be left out of this significant development.

The aim of AI projects is to develop enormously complicated smart machines that can reason, deduce, and make decisions more efficiently than "human beings."

The megabuck funding comes from large bureaucracies, federal, corporate, the military, banks, insurance firms, oil companies, space agencies, medical hospital networks. The mental tasks performed by the AI machineries include:

Expert systems that provide processed information and suggest decisions based on correlating enormous amounts of data. Here the computers perform, at almost the speed of light, the work of armies of clerks and technicians.

Voice-recognition programs; the computer recognizes instructions given in spoken languages.

Robotry.

AI has become the buzzword among investors in the computer industry. There seems little doubt that reasoning programs and robots will play increasingly important roles in Western society, and, of course, Japan.

Just as the bead game became the target of outside criticism, so has there been much grumbling about the AI movement. Some have asserted that the very term "artificial intelligence" is an oxymoron; a contradiction in terms, like "military intelligence."

Other critics point out that AI programs have little to do with individual human beings. These megamillion-dollar machines cannot be applied to solve personal problems, to help Ashley get a date on Friday night, to help Dieadra's problem with self-esteem. AI systems are designed to think like super-committees of experts. Remember the decision that it was cheaper to pay off a few large injury/death claims than to change the position of the gas tank on the Ford? Recall those Pentagon figures about "tolerable loss of civilian lives in a nuclear war"? That's why many feel that these toys of top management are more artificial than intelligent.

As it turns out, our HAL paranoias are exaggerated.

Computers will not replace real people. They will replace middle-and low-level bureaucrats. They will replace you only to the extent that you use artificial—rather than natural—intelligence in your life and work. If you think like a bureaucrat, a functionary, a manager, an unquestioning member of a large organization, or a chess player, beware: You may soon be out-thought!

Natural Intelligence

Humanists in the computer culture claim that there is only one form of intelligence natural intelligence, brain power which resides in the skulls of individual human beings. This wetware is genetically wired and experientially programmed to manage the personal affairs of one person, the owner, and to exchange thoughts with others.

All thought-processing tools, hand operated pencils, printed books, electronic computers can be used as extensions of natural intelligence. They are appliances for packaging, storing, communicating ideas: mirrors that reflect back what the user has thought. As Douglas Hofstadter put it in *Gödel Escher Bach*: "The self comes into being at the moment it has the power to reflect itself." And that power, Hesse and McLuhan, is determined by the thought tool used by the culture.

Individual human beings can be controlled, managed by thinking machines—computers or bead games—only to the extent that they voluntarily choose to censor their own independent thinking.

Magister Ludi Questions Authority

In the last chapters of *The Glass Bead Game* the hero, Joseph Knecht, has risen to the highest post in the Castalian order. He is "Magister Ludi, Master of the Glass Bead Game".

The game, by this time, has become a global artificial-intelligence system that runs the educational system, the military, science, engineering, mathematics, physics, linguistics, and above all, aesthetics. The great cultural ceremonies are public thought games watched with fascination by the populace.

At this moment of triumph the Mind Master begins to have doubts. He worries abut the two-tier-society in which the Castalian "computer" elite run the mind games of society, far removed from the realities of human life. The Castalians, we recall, have dedicated themselves totally to the life of the mind, renouncing power, money, family, individuality. A Castalian is the perfect "organization man", a monk of the new religion of artificial intelligence. Knecht is also concerned about the obedience, the loss of individual choice.

Hesse seems to be sending warning signals that are relevant to the situation in 1986. First, he suggests that human beings tend to center their religions on the thought-processing device their culture uses. The word of God has to come though normal channels or it won't be understood, from the stone tablet of Moses to the mass produced industrial product that is the "Good Book" of fundamentalist Christians and Moslems.

Second, control of the thought-processing machinery means control of society. The underlying antiestablishment tone of *The Glass Bead Game* must surely have caught the attention of George Orwell, another prophet of the information society. Like Joseph Knecht, Winston Smith, the hero of *1984*, works in the Ministry of Truth, reprogramming the master data base of history. Smith is enslaved by the information tyranny from which Hesse's hero tries to escape.

Third, Hesse suggests that the emergence of new intelligence machines will create new religions. The Castalian order is reminiscent of the mediaeval monastic cults, communities of hackers with security clearances, who knew the machine language, Latin, and who created and guarded the big mainframe illuminated manuscripts located in the palaces of bishops and dukes.

Most important, Hesse indicated the appropriate response of the individual who cannot accept the obedience and sell—renunciation demanded by the artificial—intelligence priesthood.

To Act As My Heart and Reason Command

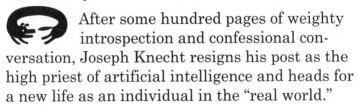 After some hundred pages of weighty introspection and confessional conversation, Joseph Knecht resigns his post as the high priest of artificial intelligence and heads for a new life as an individual in the "real world."

He explains his "awakening" in a letter to the Order. After thirty years of major league thought processing, Knecht has come to the conclusion that organizations maintain themselves by rewarding obedience with privilege! With the blinding force of a mystical experience Knecht suddenly sees that the Castalian AI community "had been infected by the characteristic disease of elite-hood-hubris, conceit, class arrogance, sell righteousness, exploitiveness. . ."!

And, irony of all irony, the member of such a thought-processing bureaucracy "often suffers from a severe lack of insight into his place in the structure of the nation, his place in the world and world history." Before we rush to smile at such platitudes about bureaucratic myopia and greed, we should remember that Hesse wrote this book during the decade when Hitler, Stalin, and Mussolini were terrorizing Europe with totalitarianism. The cliché Athenian-democratic maxim "think for yourself; question authority" was decidedly out of fashion, even in civilized countries like Switzerland.

Gentle consideration for the touchiness of the times was, we assume, the reason why Hesse, the master of parody, leads his timid readers with such a slow, formal tempo to the final confrontation between Alexander, the president of the Order, and the dissident game master. In his most courteous manner Knecht explains to Alexander that he will not accept obediently the "decision from above."

The president gasps in disbelief. And we can imagine most of the thought-processing elite of Europe, the professors, the intellectuals, the linguists, the literary critics, and news editors joining Alexander when he sputters, "not prepared to accept obediently ... an unalterable decision from above? Have I heard you right, Magister?"

Later, Alexander asks in a low voice, "And how do you act now?"

"As my heart and reason command," replies Joseph Knecht.

The best way to understand the evolution of the human race is in terms of how well we have learned to operate our brain.

8

OPERATE YOUR BRAIN

The human brain—the most infinitely and imaginatively complex knowledge system— has a hundred billion neurons, and each neuron has the knowledge-processing capacity of a powerful computer. The human brain has more connections than there are atoms in the universe. It has taken us thousands of years to even realize that we don't understand the chaotics of this complexity. The human brain can process more than a hundred million signals a second and counting.

The best way to understand the evolution of the human race is in terms of how well we have learned to operate our brain. If you think about it, we're basically brains. Our bodies are here to move our brains around. Our bodies are equipped with all these sensory inputs and output ports to bring information into the neurocomputer. In just the last decade, our species has multiplied the ability to use our brains by a thousand fold.

The way to understand how efficiently you're using your brain is to clock it in rpm—*realities per minute*. Just on the basis of input/output, my brain is now operating at a hundred times more rpm than in 1960.

When we were back in the caves a million or so years ago, we were just learning to chip stones to make tools. We lived on a planet where everything was natural. There was almost nothing artificial or even handmade—but we had the same brains. Each of our ancient ancestors carried around an enormously complex brain that eventually fissioned the atom, sent human beings to the Moon, and created rock video. Long ago we had the same brains, but we weren't using the abilities. If the brain is like a computer, then the trick is to know how to format your brain—to set up operating systems to run your brain.

If you are a computer, you have a choice. You can have word processing or not. If you have word processing, you have choices of which program to run. Once you've formatted your brain, trained your brain with that method, you have to go through that program to use it. The process of formatting your brain is called *imprinting*.

The process of formatting your brain is called imprinting.

Imprinting

Imprinting is a multimedia input of data. For a baby, it's the warmth of the mother, the softness, the sound, the taste of the breast. That's called booting up or formatting. Now baby's brain is

hooked to Mama and then of course from Mama
to Daddy, food, etc., but it's the Mama file that's
the first imprint.

There is the ability to boot up or add new
directions. To activate the brain is called *yogic*
or *psychedelic.* To transmit what's in the brain
is cybernetic. The brain, we are told by neurolo-
gist, has between seventy and a hundred buttons known as receptor sites that can imprint
different circuits. Certain biochemical—usually
botanical—products activate those particular
parts of the brain.

In tribal times, before written language,
communication was effected through the human voice, small groups, and body motion. Most
pagan tribes had rituals that occurred at harvest
time, in the springtime, or at the full Moon. The
tribe came together and activated a collective
boot-up system. They hooked all their computers
to the same tribal language. This often involved
the use of psychedelic plants.

When you think of it, the ultimate wicked
oxymoron is organized religion. Imagine a group
of control-freak men getting together and saying:
'We're going to impose our order on the fifteen-
billion-year evolutionary chaotic process that's
happening on this planet, and all over the galaxy. We're going to chisel out the rules of a bureaucracy to keep us in power."

In terms of modern computers and electronic
devices, this would be a multimedia imprinting ceremony. The fire was the center of light
and heat. There were symbolic objects, such
as feathers or bones. This experience booted up

A human being is basically a tribal person, the brains of all present so they could share the basic tribal system. But each person could have his own vision quest. He could howl like a wolf, hoot like an owl, roll around like a snake. Each tribal member was learning how to activate, operate, boot up, and accept the uniqueness of his/her own brain.

A human being is basically a tribal person, most comfortable being together in small groups facilitating acceptance and understanding of each other as individuals. Later forms of civilization have discredited individualism. The history of the evolution of the human spirit has to do with new methods of media, communication, or language.

Communication Control

About five thousand years ago, after the species got pretty good with tools and building, somewhere in the Middle East—possibly also in China—people began making marks on shells and on pieces of papyrus. This allowed for long-distance communication. Handwriting, which linked up hundreds of thousands of people, gave total power to the people who knew how to control the writing. Marshall McLuhan reminded us that throughout human history, whoever controls the media controls the people. This is French semiotics. Literacy is used to control the poor. The educated use literacy to control the uneducated.

A typical feudal organization, such as the Catholic Church, restricted the power to send a message like this to a very special class of computer hacker-nerds called monks. Only they were authorized to touch the mainframe—the illuminated manuscripts up in the castle of the duke or cardinal. But to the others—no matter how important a person in the village or the city—the word came down from the Higher Ups.

Once people start organizing in large groups of thousands, or hundreds of thousands, the tribal situation could no longer be controlled. If a hundred thousand people are all hooked up, like a hive or termite colony, there has to be some central organization that keeps it going.

With thousands of people carrying rocks to build a pyramid, or thousands of people building the churches of the pope, a feudal society can't function if the workers are accessing their singular brain programs. To illustrate the totalitarian power control of the feudal situation, consider the basic metaphor of the "shepherd" and the "sheep." "The Lord is my shepherd; I shall not want. He maketh me to he down in green pastures." Now, if the Lord is your shepherd, who the fuck are you? Bah! Even today, when the pope flies around to third-world countries, they speak of "the pope and his flock."

Bible as Brain Control

Another example of brain control preventing the individual from accessing his or her own computer is the first chapter of the *Bible*. The opening text of Genesis lays it right out. God says,

"I made the skies. I made the planets, I made the earth, I made the water, I made the land. I made the creepy-crawly things, and I made you, Adam, to be in my likeness, and I put you in the ultimate destination resort, which is the Garden of Eden. Boy, you can do anything you want. I'm going to pull out a rib and give you a helpmate like a little kitchen slave, named Eve. You can do whatever you want, Adam. This is paradise.

"However, there are two Food and Drug regulations. See that tree over there? That's the Tree of Immortality. It offers cryonics and cloning. You shall not eat of the fruit of that lest you become a God like me and live forever. You see that tree over there. That's even more dangerous. You shall not eat of the fruit of that because that is the Tree of Knowledge. It offers expansions of consciousness."

Genesis makes it clear that the whole universe is owned, operated, controlled, and fabricated by one God—and he's a big, bad-tempered male. That's why we have a war on mind drugs. The one thing that no mass society can stand is individuals and small groups that go off to start learning how to program, reprogram, boot up, activate, and format their own brains.

There's a good reason for these taboos. The feudal and industrial stages of evolution are similar to the stages in the evolution of individuals. Young children are glad to have Daddy be shepherd, but after a while the child has to take responsibility.

Feudal societies imprinted millions to totally devote their lives to being herd flock animals, imagine living on a farm fifty miles from Chartres during the 15th Century. On Sundays you walked five miles to get to a little village. There the priest told you, "Listen, six months from now we're all going to Chartres. There's going to be a big ceremony because the archbishop will be there."

The one thing that no mass society can stand is individuals and small groups that go off to start learning how to program, reprogram, boot up, activate, and format their own brains.

You spent a week to hike there. You walked into the central square of Chartres. You looked up and saw a cathedral taller than any trees, almost like a mountain, with its stained-glass windows and statues, and there were all those people the priest told you about. They're seven or ten feet tall. You walked in, looked up at the towering Gothic arches, the rose windows, heard the organ music and chanting, smelled the incense.

Talk about multi-sensory, multimedia imprinting! If you thought that the Grateful Dead light show was something, for almost two thousand years the wizards of the Catholic Church orchestrated one hell of a show. The smell of perfume, the candles, the chanting getting louder and louder, until suddenly the bishop appeared, bejeweled, carried in on a big golden throne. You'd never seen anything like that back on the farm.

An earlier multimedia imprinting event took place near Athens before the birth of Christ. The Eleusinian mystery rite was an annual religious event that reoccurred for over a thousand years. The wisest people as well as ordinary folk came

You create the realities you inhabit. to the temple of Eleusis to participate in the secret ceremony. An LSD-type drink made from ergot of barley was drunk by all the initiates. An extravagant light show and a powerful dramatic reenactment was performed, resulting in a group experience of chaos and rebirth for the audience.

It's no accident that the Greek philosophers, dramatists, and poets left an incredible record of creative self-expression and polytheism. When Socrates said, "The function of human life is to know yourself; intelligence is virtue," he was invoking the Greek notion of humanism that was to later influence the Renaissance and the romantic periods.

Far more than by weapons, society is controlled by multimedia, neurological imprinting. Marshall McLuhan reminded us that the medium is the message.

When Gutenberg invented moveable type, it empowered dukes and cardinals to print and distribute thousands of Bibles and histories of the Crown. Within a few decades, many Europeans were learning how to do what only the monks could do. Gutenberg created the one device that was basic to the future industrial—factory civilization—mass production for consumers.

In the industrial age, the virtuous person was good, prompt, reliable, dependable, efficient, directed, and, of course, replaceable. There was not much need for the individual to operate his or her own brain in a factory civilization. The bosses can't have people on an assembly line becoming too creative, as in the Cheech and Chong movie where cars are coming down the line.

Cheech & Chong Workin'

Hey, Cheech, I'm gonna go eat now."
"You can't, not yet." "Why not?"
"You can't eat until the bell rings."
"Okay, let's paint the next car rainbow."

You cannot operate industrial society with too much individuality and access to the multimedia capacities of the brain.

Around 1900 Einstein came up with the idea that space and time only exist in an interactive field, and Max Planck devised a theory that the basic elements of the universe are particles of information. Then came Heisenberg's proof that you create your own reality. And a new philosophy emerged called *quantum physics*, which suggests that the individual's function is to inform and be informed. You really exist only when you're in a field sharing and exchanging information. You create the realities you inhabit.

What's the brain for? Why do we have this incredible instrument? Our brains want to be hooked up with other brains. My brain is only in operation when she's slamming back and forth bytes and bits of information. Multimedia intercommunication.

The original basic dream of humanity is that the individual has divinity within. There is this enormous power within our bio-computer brains. We are going to have to learn how to use this power, how to boot it up.

9

BOOT UP YOUR BIO-COMPUTER

The human brain, we are told, is a galaxy
of over a hundred billion neurons, any two of
which can organize and communicate as much
complex information as a mainframe computer.

Many cognitive psychologists now see the
brain as a universe of information processors.
Our minds, according to this metaphor, serve
as the software that programs the neural hardware—or wetware. Most of the classic psychological terms can now be redefined in terms
of computer concepts. Cognitive functions like
memory, forgetting, learning, creativity, and
logical thinking are now studied as methods by
which the mind forms "data bases" and stores,
processes, shuffles, and retrieves information.

Noncognitive functions such as emotions,
moods, sensory perceptions, hallucinations,
obsessions, phobias, altered states, possession
trance experiences, glossolalias, intoxications,
visionary images, and psychedelic perspectives
can now be viewed in terms of ROM brain circuits or autonomous-sympathetic-midbrain sectors that are usually not accessed by left-brain

or forebrain conscious decision. These nonlinear, unconscious areas can, as we well know, be activated intentionally or involuntarily by various means. The pop term "turn on" carries the fascinating cybernetic implication that one can selectively dial up or access brain sectors that process specific channels of information signals normally unavailable.

These concepts could emerge only in an electronic culture. The mystics and altered-state philosophers of the past, like the Buddha or St. John of the Cross or William James or Aldous Huxley, could not describe their visions and illuminations and ecstasies and enlightenments in terms of "turning on" electronic appliances.

Computers Help Understand the Brain

There is no naïve assumption here that the brain is a computer. However, by using cybernetic terminology to describe mind and brain functions, we can add to our knowledge about the varieties of thought-processing experiences.

This use of a manufactured artifact like the computer to help us understand internal biological processes seems to be a normal stage in the growth of human knowledge. Harvey's notions about the heart as pump and the circulation of the blood obviously stemmed from hydraulic engineering. Our understanding of metabolism and nutrition inside the body had to await the science of thermodynamics and energy machines.

Two hundred years ago, before electrical appliances were commonplace, the brain was vaguely defined as an organ that secreted "thoughts" the way the heart processed blood and the lungs processed air. In the 1950s my Psychology 101 professors described the brain in terms of the most advanced information system available—an enormous telephone exchange. This metaphor obviously did not lead to profitable experimentation; so the brain was generally ignored by psychology. The psychoanalytic theories of Freud were more useful and comprehensible, because they were based on familiar thermodynamic principles: Neurosis was caused by the blocking or repression of surging, steamy, over-heated dynamic instincts that exploded or leaked out in various symptomatic behavior.

During the early Sixties our Harvard Psychedelic Drug Research project studied the reactions of thousands of subjects during psilocybin and LSD sessions. We were able to recognize and classify the standard range of psychedelic-hallucinogenic experiences, and to distinguish them from the effects of other drugs like uppers, downers, booze, opiates, tranquilizers. But we were able to categorize them only in terms of subjective reactions. There was simply no scientific language to communicate or model for the wide range and "strange" effects of these chaotic phenomena. Psychiatrists, policemen, moralists, and people who did not use drugs accepted the notion of "psychotomimetic states." There was one normal way to see the world. Chaotic drugs caused all users to lose their grasp on the one-and-only authorized reality, thus mimicking insanity.

Looking to Mysticism

To talk and think about drug-induced experiences, the Harvard drug experimenters and other researchers were forced to fall back on the ancient literature of Christian mysticism and those oriental yogic disciplines that had studied visionary experiences for centuries. The scholars of mysticism and spiritual transcendence snobbishly tended to view "normal reality" as a web of socially induced illusions. They tended to define, as the philosophic religious goal of life, the attainment of altered states.

Needless to say, enormous confusion was thus created. Most sensible, practical Americans were puzzled and irritated by this mad attempt on the part of the mystical millions to enthusiastically embrace chemical insanity and self-induced chaotics. Epistemological debates about the definition of reality soon degenerated into hysterical social extremism on the part of almost all concerned, present company included. Arguments about the nature of reality are always heavy, often bitter and emotional. Cultural, moral, political, racial, and above all, generational issues were involved in the Drug Wars of the late 20th Century.

But the basic problem was semiotic. Debate collapsed into emotional babble because there was no language or conceptual model of what happened when you got "high", "stoned", "fucked up", loaded", "wasted", "blessed", "spaced out", "illuminated", "satirized," "god-intoxicated", etc.

Those young, bright baby-boom Americans, who had been dialing and tuning television screens since infancy, and who had learned how to activate and turn on their brains using chaotic drugs in serious introspective experiments, were uniquely prepared to engineer the interface between the computer and the cybernetic organ known as the human brain.

Here again, external technology can provide us with an updated model and language to understand inner neuro-function. Television became popularized in the 1950s. Many psychedelic trippers of the next decades tended to react like television viewers passively watching the pictures flashing on their mind-screens. The semantic level of the acid experimenters was defined by the word "Wow!" The research groups I worked with at Harvard, Millbrook, and Berkeley fell back on gaseous, oriental, Genges-enlightenment terminology for which I humbly apologize.

Then, in the Seventies, the Apple computer was introduced. At the same time video games, provided young people with a hands-on experience of moving flashy electronic, digital information around on screens. It was no accident that many of the early designers and marketers of these electronic appliances lived in the San Francisco area and tended to be intelligent adepts in the use of psychedelic drugs.

Those young, bright baby-boom Americans, who had been dialing and tuning television screens since infancy, and who had learned how to activate and turn on their brains using chaotic drugs in serious introspective experiments, were uniquely prepared to engineer the interface between the computer and the cybernetic organ known as the human brain. They could handle accelerated thought-processing, multilevel realities, instantaneous chains of digital logic much more comfortably than their less-playful, buttoned-up, conservative, MBA rivals at IBM. Much of Steve Jobs's astonishing success in developing the Apple and the MAC was explicitly motivated by his crusade against IBM, seen as the archenemy of the 1960s culture.

In the Eighties, millions of young Americans became facile in digital thought-processing using inexpensive home computers. Most of them intuitively understood that the best model for understanding and operating the mind came from the mix of psychedelic and cybernetic cultures.

Hundreds of New-Age pop psychologists, like Werner Erhard and Shirley MacLane, taught folks how to re-program their minds, write the scripts of their lives, upgrade thought-processing. At the same time the new theories of imprinting, i.e., sudden programming of the brain, were popularized by ethologists and hip psychologists like Conrad Lorenz, Niko Tinbergen, and John Lilly.

Once again, external engineered tools helped us understand inner function. If the brain is viewed as bio-hardware, and psychedelic drugs become "neurotransmitters," and if you can reprogram your mind, for better or for worse, by "turning on", then

It was no accident that many of the early designers and marketers of these electronic appliances lived in the San Francisco area and tended to be intelligent adepts in the use of psychedelic drugs, new concepts and techniques of instantaneous psychological change become possible.

Another relevant question arises. Can the computer screen create altered states? Is there a digitally induced 'high'? Can psychedelic electrons be packaged like chemicals to strike terror into the heart of the White House? Do we need a Digital Enforcement Agency (DEA) to teach kids to say "No", or more politely, "No, thank you" to RAM pushers?

My opinion is in the negative. But what do I know? I am currently enjoying a mild digital dependence, but it seems manageable and socially useful. I follow the ancient Sufi-Pythagorean maxim regarding creative writing:

> *"If thou write stoned, edit straight. If thou write straight, edit stoned."*

........and always with a team.

10

CYBERFREEDOM

Once upon a time ... knowledge-information was stored in extremely expensive mainframe systems called illuminated volumes, usually Bibles, carefully guarded in the palace of the duke or bishop, and accessible only to security-cleared, socially-alienated hackers called monks. Then in 1456 Johannes Gutenberg invented a most important piece of hardware: the moveable-type printing press. This knowledge-information processing system could mass-produce inexpensive, portable software readily available for home use: The Personal Book.

Until recently, computers were in much the same sociopolitical situation as the pre-Gutenberg systems.The mainframe knowledge-processors that ran society were the monopoly of governments and large corporations. They were carefully guarded by priestly technicians with security clearances. The average person, suddenly thrust into electronic illiteracy and digital helplessness, was understandably threatened.

The Mainframe Monopoly

My first contact with computers came in 1950, when I was director of a Kaiser Foundation psychological research project that developed mathematical profiles for the inter-personal assessment of personality. In line with the principles of humanistic psychology the aim of this research was to free persons from depen-dency on doctors, professionals, institutions, and diagnostic-thematic interpretations. To this end, we elicited clusters of yes-no responses form subjects and fed back knowledge in the from of profiles and indices to the patients themselves.

Relying on dimensional information rather than interpretative categories, our research was ideally suited to computer analysis. Routinely we sent stacks of data to the Kaiser Foundation's computer room, where mysterious technicians con-verted our numbers into relevant indices. Comput-ers were thus helpful, but distant and unapproach-able. I distrusted the mainframes because I saw them as devices that would merely increase the dependence of individuals upon experts.

In 1960 I became a director of the Harvard Psychedelic Drug Research program. The aims of this project were also humanistic: to teach individuals how to self-administer psychoac-tive drugs in order to free their psyches without reliance upon doctors or institutions. Again we used mainframes to index responses to question-naires about drug experiences, but I saw no way for this awesome knowledge-power to be put in the hands of individuals. I know now that our research with psychedelic drugs and, in fact, the drug culture itself was a forecast of, or preparation for, the personal-computer age. Indeed, it was a brilliant LSD researcher, John Lilly, who in 1972 wrote the seminal monograph on the brain as a knowledge-information processing system: *Programming and Metaprogramming in the Human Biocomputer*. Psychedelic drugs expose one to the raw experience of chaotic brain function, with the protections of the mind temporarily suspended. We are talking here about the tremendous acceleration of images, the crumbling of analogic perceptions into vapor trails of neuron off-on flashes, the multiplication of disorderly mind programs slipping in and out of awareness like floppy disks.

The seven million Americans who experienced the awesome potentialities of the brain via LSD certainly paved the way for the computer society. It is no accident that the term "LSD" was used twice in *Time* magazine's cover story about Steve Jobs, for it was Jobs and his fellow Gutenberger, Stephen Wozniak, who hooked up the personal brain with the personal computer and thus made a new culture possible.

Hands On/Tune In

The development of the personal computer was a step of Gutenberg magnitude. Just as The Personal Book transformed formed human society from the muscular-feudal to the mechanical-industrial, so has the personal electronic-knowledge processor equipped the individual to survive and evolve into the age of information. To guide us in this confusing and scary transition, it is most useful to look back and see what happened during the Gutenberg mutation. Religion was the unifying force that held feudal society together. It was natural, therefore, that the first Personal Books would be Bibles. When the religion market was satiated, many entrepreneurs wondered what other conceivable use could be made of this newfangled software.

How-to-read books were the next phase. Then came game books. It is amusing to note that the second book printed in the English language was on chess—a game that became, with its knights and bishops and kings and queens, the Pac Man of late feudalism. We can see this same pattern repeating during the current transition. Since money/business is the unifying force of the industrial age, the first Wozniak bibles were, naturally enough, accounting spreadsheets. Then came word processors, and games.

The history of human evolution is the record of technological innovation. Expensive machinery requiring large group efforts for operation generally becomes a tool of social repression by the state. The tower clock. The galley ship. The cannon. The tank. Instruments that can be owned and operated by individuals inevitably produce democratic revolutions. The bronze dagger. The crossbow. The pocket watch. The automobile as self-mover. This is the liberating "hands-on" concept. "Power to the people" means personal technology available to the individual. D.I.Y.— Do It Yourselves.

Evolution/Revolution

Digital-graphic appliances are developing a partnership between human brains and computers. In evolving to more physiological complexity, our bodies formed symbioses with armies of digestive bacteria necessary for survival. In similar fashion, our brains are forming neural-electronic symbiotic linkups with solid-state computers.

It is useful to distinguish here between addictions and symbiotic partnerships. The body can become passively addicted to certain molecules, e.g., of heroin, and the brain can become passively addicted to electronic signals, e.g., from television. The human body, as we have noted, also requires symbiotic partnerships with certain unicellular organisms.

At this point in human evolution, more and more people are developing mutually dependent, interactive relationships with their microsystems. When this happens, there comes a moment when the individual is "hooked" and cannot imagine living without the continual interchange of electronic signals between the personal brain and the personal computer.

There are interesting political implications. In the near future, more than twenty million Americans will use computers to establish intense interactive

If we are to stay free, we must see to it that the right to own digital data processors becomes as inalienable as the constitutional guarantees of free speech and a free press.

partnerships with other inhabitants of cyberspace. These individuals will operate at a level
of intelligence that is qualitatively different from
those who use static forms of knowledge-information processing. In America, this difference is
already producing a generation gap, i.e., a species
gap. After Gutenberg, Personal Books created a
new level of individual thinking that revolution-
ized society. An even more dramatic mutation in
human intelligence will occur as the new digital
light appliances permit individuals to communicate with individuals in other lands

Childhood's End?

It seems clear that we are facing one of
those genetic crossroads that have occurred so frequently in the history of primates.
The members of the human gene pool who form
symbiotic links with solid state computers will
be characterized by extremely high individual
intelligence and will settle in geographic niches
that encourage individual access to knowledge-
information-processing software.

New associations of individuals linked by
computers will surely emerge. Information nets
will encourage a swift, free interchange among
individuals. Feedback peripherals will dramatically expand the mode of exchange from keyboard
punching to neurophysiological interaction.

The keyword is, of course, "interaction." The
intoxicating power of interactive software is
that it eliminates dependence on the enormous
bureaucracy of knowledge professionals that
flourished in the industrial age. In the factory

culture, guilds and unions and associations of knowledge-workers jealously monopolized the flow of information. Educators, teachers, professors, consultants, psychotherapists, librarians, managers, journalists, editors, writers, labor unions, medical groups all such roles are now threatened.

It is not an exaggeration to speculate about the development of very different postindustrial societies. Solid-state literacy will be almost universal in America and the other Western democracies. The rest of the world, especially the totalitarian countries, will be kept electronically illiterate by their rulers. At least half the United Nations' members now prohibit or limit personal possession. And, as the implications of personal computers become more clearly understood, restrictive laws will become more apparent. If we are to stay free, we must see to it that the right to own digital data processors becomes as inalienable as the constitutional guarantees of free speech and a free press.

> **If we are to stay free, we must see to it that the right to own digital data processors becomes as inalienable as the constitutional guarantees of free speech and a free press.**

Psychedelic drugs expose one to the raw experience of chaotic brain function, with the protections of the mind temporarily suspended. We are talking here about the tremendous acceleration of images, the crumbling of analogic perceptions into vapor trails of neuron off-on flashes, the multiplication of disorderly mind programs slipping in and out of awareness like floppy disks.

11

QUANTUM JUMPS

The great philosophic achievement of the 20th Century was the discovery, made by nuclear and quantum physicists around 1900, that the visible tangible reality is written in BASIC. We seem to inhabit a universe made up of a small number of elements particles bits that swirl in chaotic clouds, occasionally clustering together in geometrically logical temporary configurations.

The solid Newtonian universe involving such immutable concepts as mass, force, momentum, and inertia, all bound into a Manichaean drama involving equal reactions of good versus evil, gravity versus levity, and entropy versus evolution, produced such pious Bank of England notions as conservation of energy. This General Motors's universe, which was dependable, dull, and predictable, became transformed in the hands of Einstein/Planck into digitized, shimmering quantum screens of electronic probabilities.

Chalk: A soft, white, grey, or buff limestone composed chiefly of the shells of foraminifers.

Quantum: The quantity or amount of something; an indivisible unit of energy; the particle mediating a specific type of elemental interaction.

Quantum Jump: Any abrupt change or step, especially in knowledge or information.

Chaos: The basic state of the universe and the human brain.

Personal Computer: A philosophic digital appliance that allows the individual to operate and communicate in the quantum information age.

By the end of the 20th century we were navigating in a reality of which Niels Bohr and Werner Heisenberg could only dream, and which Marshall McLuhan predicted. It turns out that the universe described in their psychedelic equations is best understood as a super mainframe constellation of information processor with subprograms and temporary ROM states, macros called galaxies, stars; minis called planets; micros called organisms; metamicros known as molecules, atoms, particles; and, last, but not least, micros called Macintosh.

It seems to follow that the great technological challenge of the 20th Century was to produce an inexpensive appliance that would make the chaotic universe "user friendly," which would allow the individual human to digitize, store, process, and reflect the subprograms that make up his/her own personal realities

Murmur the name "Einstein," put your hand reverently on your mouse, and give it an admiring pat. Your modest, faithful, devoted Mac is an evolutionary celebrity! It may be an advance as important as the opposable thumb, face to face lovemaking, the Model T Ford, the printing press! Owning it defines you as member of a new breed—postindustrial, postbiological, posthuman—because your humble VM (Volks-Mac) permits you to think and act in terms of clusters of electrons. It allows you to cruise around in the chaotic post-Newtonian information ocean, to think and communicate in the lingua franca of the universe, the binary dialect of galaxies and atoms. Light.

A Philosophic Appliance

The chain of events that elevated us to this new genetic status, Homo sapiens electronicus, began around the turn of the century.

Physicists are traditionally assigned the task of sorting out the nature of reality. So it was Einstein, Planck, Heisenberg, Bohr, et al., who figured out that the units of energy/matter were subatomic particles that zoom around in clouds of ever changing, off-on, 0-1, yin-yang probabilities.

Einstein and the quantum physicists digitized our universe, reduced our solid realities into clusters of pixels, into recursive stairways of Godel-Escher-Bach paradox. No one understood, at first, what they were talking about. They

Quantum physics is quite literally a wild acid. trip!

expressed their unsettling theories in complex equations written on blackboards with chalk. These great physicists thought and communicated with a neolithic tool: chalk marks on the blackboard of the cave. The paradox was this: Einstein and his brilliant colleagues could not experience or operate or communicate at a quantum electronic level. In a sense they were idiot savants, able to produce equations about chaos and relativity without being able to maintain interpersonal cyberrelationships with others.

Imagine if Max Planck, paddling around in his chalkboard skin-canoe, had access to a video arcade game! He'd see right away that the blips on Centipede and the zaps of Space invaders could represent the movement of the particles that he tried to describe in chalk-dust symbols on his blackboard.

Reflect on the head-aching adjustment required here. The universe described by Einstein and the nuclear physicists is alien and terrifying. Chaotic. Quantum physics is quite literally a wild acid trip! It postulates a hallucinatory Alice-in-Wonderland universe in which everything is changing. As Heisenberg and Jimi Hendrix said, "Nothing is certain except uncertainty." Matter is energy. Energy is matter at various forms of acceleration. Particles dissolve into waves. There is no up or down in a four-dimensional movie. It all depends on your attitude, i.e., your angle of approach to the real worlds of chaotics.

In 1910, the appliance we call the universe was not user friendly and there was no hands-on manual of operations. No wonder people felt helpless and superstitious. People living in the solid, mechanical world of 1910 could no more understand or experience an Einsteinian universe than Queen Victoria could levitate or fish could read and write English. Einstein was denounced as evil and immoral by Catholic bishops and sober theologians who sensed how unsettling and revolutionary these new ideas could be.

In retrospect we see that the first seventy five years of the 20th Century were devoted to preparing, training, and initiating human beings to communicate in quantum speak, i.e., to think and act at an entirely different level in terms of digital clusters.

The task of preparing human culture for new realities has traditionally been performed by tribal communicators called artists, entertainers, performers. When Greek philosophers came up with notions of humanism, individuality, and liberty, it was the painters and sculptors of Athens who produced the commercial logos, the naked statues of curvy Venus and sleek Mercury and the other randy Olympian Gods.

When the feudal, anti-human monotheisms—Christian-Islamic—took over, it was the "nerdy" monks and

> The task of preparing human culture for new realities has traditionally been performed by tribal communicators called artists, entertainers, performers.

painters who produced the commercial artwork of
the Middle Ages. God as a bearded king swathed
in robes. Madonna and Bleeding Saints and cruci-
fied Jesus, wall-to-wall anguished martyrs. These
advertising logos were necessary, of course, to
convince the serfs to submit to the All Powerful
Lord. You certainly can't run a kingdom or empire
with bishops, popes, cardinals, abbots, and chan-
cellors of the exchequer joyously running around
bare-assed like Athenian pantheists.

The Renaissance was a humanist revival preparing Europeans for the industrial age. When
Gutenberg invented the cheap, portable, rag-
and-glue home computer known as the printing press, individuals had to be encouraged to
read and write and "do it yourself!" Off came the
clothes! Michelangelo erected a statue of David,
naked as a jay bird, in the main square of Flor-
ence. Why David? He was the young, punk kid
who stood up against Goliath, the Wed Rambo
hit man of the Philistine empire.

With this historical perspective we can see
that the 20th Century produced an avalanche
of artistic, literary, musical, and entertainment
movements, all of which shared the same goal: to
strip off the robes and uniforms; to dissolve our
blind faith in static structure; to loosen up the ri-
gidities of the industrial culture; to prepare us to
deal with paradox, with altered states of perception, with multidimensional definitions of nature;
to make quantum reality comfortable, manageable, homey, livable; to get you to feel at home
while bouncing electrons around your computer
screen. Radio. Telegraph. Television. Computers.

Digital Art: Do It Yourself!

In modern art we saw the emergence of schools that dissolved reality representation into a variety of subjective, relativistic attitudes. Impressionists used random spots of color and brush strokes, converting matter to reflected light waves. Seurat and the Pointillists actually painted in pixels.

Expressionism offered a quantum reality that was almost totally spontaneous. Do It Yourself! (D.I.Y.) Cubism sought to portray common objects in planes and volumes reflecting the underlying geometric structure of matter, thus directly illustrating the new physics. The Dada and collage movements broke up material reality into diverse bits and bytes.

Surrealism produced a slick, smooth-plastic fake reality that was later perfected by Sony. In Tokyo I have listened to electronic anthropologists argue that Dali's graphic "The Persistence of Memory"—featuring melting watches—created modern Japanese culture, which no one can deny is eminently surreal.

These avant garde aesthetic D.I.Y. experiments were quickly incorporated into pop art, advertising, and industrial design. Society was learning to live with the shifting-screen perspectives and pixillated representations of the universe that had been predicted by the equations of the quantum physicists. When the Coca-Cola company uses the digitized face of Max Headroom as its current logo, then America is comfortably living in a quantum universe.

Hacking Away at the Word Line

These same aesthetic trends appeared in English literature. Next time you boot up your Mac, breathe a word of gratitude to Emerson, Stein, Yeats, Pound, Huxley, Beckett, Orwell, Burroughs, Gysin—all of whom succeeded in loosening social, political, religious linearities, and encouraging subjectivity and innovative reprogramming of chaotic realities.

The most influential literary work of this period was produced by James Joyce. In *Ulysses* and *Finnegans Wake*, Joyce fissioned and sliced the grammatical structure of language into thoughtbytes. Joyce was not only a writer, but also a word processor, a protohacker, reducing ideas to elemental units and endlessly recombining them at will. Joyce programmed reality using his own basic language, a quantum linguistic that allowed him to assemble and reassemble thoughts into fugal, repetitious, contrapuntal patterns. It helped that he was semi-blind and dyslexic.)

Imagine what James Joyce could have done with MS Word or a CD-ROM graphic system or a modern data base! Well, we don't have to imagine—he actually managed to do it using his own brainware.

Jazz

The most effective pre-computer rendition of quantum-digital art was to be found in a certain low-life high-tech style of spontaneous, cool, subjective, improvisational sound waves produced by a small group of black audio engineers. Jazz suddenly popped up at the height of the industrial age, eroding its linear values and noninteractive styles. A factory society demands regularity, dependability, replicability, predictability, conformity. There is no room for improvisation or syncopated individuality on a Newtonian assembly line; so it

> There is no room for improvisation or syncopated individuality on a Newtonian assembly line.

was left to the African-Americans, who never really bought the factory culture, to get us boogying into the postindustrial quantum age. Needless to say, the moralists instinctively denounced jazz as chaotic, low life, and vaguely sinful.

Radio

The most important factor in preparing a society of assembly-line workers and factory managers for the quantum information age was the invention of a user-friendly electronic appliance called radio.

Radio is the communication of audible signals, such as words or music, encoded in electromagnetic waves. Radio allows us to package and transmit ideas in digital patterns. The first use of "wireless" was by government, military, and business, but within one generation the home micro radio allowed the individual to turn on and tune in a range of realities.

When Farmer Jones learned how to select stations by moving the dial, he had taken the first hands-on step toward the information age. By 1936 the comforting sounds of Amos 'n' Andy and swing music had prepared human beings for the magic of quantum electronic communication, as well as the brainwashing powers of political leaders.

Movies Project Realities onto Screens

The next step in creating an electronic computer culture was a big one. Light waves passed through celluloid frames projected life like images on screens, producing new levels of reality that transformed human thought and communication.

It was a big step when computer designers decided to output data on screens instead of those old green-white Gutenberg printouts. The silent movies made this innovation possible. It is, perhaps, no accident that in the 1980s IBM used the lovable, irresistible icon of the Little Tramp in its commercials.

The next time you direct your hypnotized eyeballs toward your lit-up terminal, remember that it was cheerful Charlie Chaplin who first accustomed our species to accept the implausible quantum reality of electrical impulses flashing on a flat screen.

TV Brought the Language of Electrons into Our Homes

World War II was the first high tech war. It was fought on electronic screens: radar, sonar. The Allied victory was enormously aided by Alan Turing, the father of artificial intelligence, who used primitive computers to crack the German codes.

As soon as the war was over, these new technologies became available for civilian use. There is simply no way that a culture of television addicts can comprehend or appreciate the changes in human psychology brought about by the boob tube.

The average American spends more time
per week watching television than in any other
social activity. Pixels dancing on a screen are the
central reality. People spend more time gazing
at electrons than they do gazing into the eyes
of their loved ones, looking into books, scanning
other aspects of material reality. Talk about applied metaphysics! Electronic reality is more real
than the physical world! This is a profound evolutionary leap. It can be compared to the jump
from ocean to shoreline, when land and air
suddenly become more real to the ex-fish
than water!

Television Passivity

The first generation of television watching produced a nation of "vidiots"—passive amoeboids
sprawled in front of the feeding-screen sucking
up digital information. Giant networks controlled the airwaves, hawking commercial products and packaged politics like carnival snake oil
salesmen.

Perceptive observers realized that Orwell's
nightmare of a Big Brother society was too
optimistic. In *1984* the authoritarian state used
television to spy on citizens. The actuality is
much worse: citizens docilely, voluntarily lin-
ing themselves up in front of the authority box,
enjoying the lethal, neurological fast food dished
out in technicolour by Newspeak.

Visionary prophets like Marshall McLuhan
understood what was happening. He said, "The
medium is the message." Never mind about
the junk on the screen. That will change and

improve. The point is that people are receiving signals on the screen. McLuhan knew that the new electronic technology would create the new global language when the time was ripe, i.e., when society had been prepared to take this quantum leap.

Computer Passivity

The first generations of computer users similarly did not understand the nature of the quantum revolution. Top management saw computers as Invaluable Business Machines[TL]. Computers simply produced higher efficiency by replacing muscular-factory-clerical labor.

And the rest of us—recognizing in the 1960s that computers in the hands of the managers would increase their power to manipulate and control us—developed a fear and loathing of computers.

Some sociologists with paranoid survival tendencies have speculated that this phobic revulsion against electronic communication shared by millions of college-educated, liberal book readers was deliberately created by Counter Intelligence Authorities[TL], whose control would be eroded by widespread electronic literacy.

The plot further thickened when countercultural code-cowgirls and code-cowboys, combining the insights and liberated attitudes of beats, hippies, acidheads, rock 'n' rollers, hackers, cyberpunks, and electronic visionaries, rode into Silicon Valley and foiled the great brain robbery by developing the great equalizer: the Personal Computer.

The birth of the information age occurred in 1976, not in a smoky industrial town like Bethlehem, PA, but in a

> **Freedom in any country is measured by the percentage of personal computers in the hands of individuals?**

humble manger—garage—in sunny, postindustrial Silicon Valley. The Personal Computer was invented by two bearded, long-haired guys, St. Stephen the Greater and St. Steven the Lesser. And to complete the biblical metaphor, the infant prodigy was named after the Fruit of the Tree of Knowledge: the Apple! The controlled substance with which Eve committed the first original sin: Thinking for Herself!

The Personal Computer triggered a new round of confrontation in the age-old social-political competition: control by the state and individual freedom of thought. Remember how the Athenian PCs, goaded by code-cowboys like Socrates and Plato, hurled back the mainframes of the Spartans and the Persians? Remember how the moveable-type press in private hands printed out the hard copy that overthrew theocratic control of the papacy and later disseminated the Declaration of Independence? Is it not true that freedom in any country is measured perfectly by the percentage of Personal Computers in the hands of individuals?

Role of the Free Agent

Those who like to think for themselves—free agents—tend to see computers as thought-appliances. "Appliance" defines a device that individuals use in the home for their own comfort, entertainment, or education.

What are the applications of a thought-appliance? Self-improvement? Self-education. Home entertainment? Mind interplay with friends? Thought games? Mental fitness? Significant pursuits?

Free agents use their minds not to perform authorized duties for the soviet state or the International Bureaucracy Machine[TL] but for anything that damn well suits their fancies as Americans. In the old industrial civilization you called yourself a worker, but in the information age you're a free agent. As you develop your agency, you develop your skills in communication.

Personal Computer Owners are Discovering That the Brain is:

•◆ The ultimate organ for pleasure and awareness;

•◆ An array of a hundred billion micro-computers waiting to be booted up, activated, stimulated, and programmed;

•◆ Waiting impatiently for software, headware, thoughtware that pays respect to its awesome potential and makes possible electronic internet linkage with other brains.

12

FROM YIPPIES TO YUPPIES

Before 1946, youngsters absorbed and joined their culture by means of personal observation of significant grown ups. You watched the neighborhood doctor and the local carpenter and the nurse or the maiden aunt, and you drifted into a job. Books, sermons, magazine articles about heroic or antisocial figures also helped define the nature of the social game.

Television changed all that. The average American household watches television more than seven hours a day. This statistic means that yuppies learned about culture, absorbed the roles, rules, rituals, styles, and jargon of the game, not from personal observation but from television images. The cartoons, soap operas, prime time dramas, and game shows tend to be escapist. The news broadcasts tend to feature victims and righteous whiners rather than successful role models. Politicians reciting rehearsed lies are not seen as credible heroes.

The only aspect of television that presents real people engaged in actions that are existentially true, credible, and scientifically objective are the sportscasts. This may explain the enormous media attention given to organized athletics. The average kid watches Fernando Valenzuela or Joe Montana or Kareem Abdul Jabbar perform and is then exposed to endless interviews with and stories about these successful, self-made professionals. Their opinions, moods, physical ailments, philosophies, and lifestyles are presented in microscopic detail. People know more about Larry Bird as a "real person" than they do about Walter Mondale or George Bush or Dan Rather.

Any predictions about the future that the yuppies created was based on the fact that they were the first members of the information communication culture. It is inevitable that they would become more realistic, more professional, more skilled. Intelligence was their ethos and their model. They understand that the smart thing to do was to construct a peaceful, fair, just, compassionate social order.

Enter Yuppies

After my deportation from Harvard University many years ago, I was, among other things, a freelance college professor paid by students for one-night-stand lectures about topics too hot for salaried professors.

Back in the Sixties when I flew in for a lecture, the student committee showed up at the airport wearing long hair, sandals, blue jeans, and cheerful, impudent grins. The radio would be blasting out Mick Jagger and Jimi Hendrix as we drove to the campus. The students eagerly asked me about "high" technologies—methods of consciousness expansion, new brands of wonder drugs, new forms of protest, up-to-date developments in the ever-changing metaphysical philosophies of rock stars: Yoko Ono's theory of astrology; Peter Townsend's devotion to Baba Ram Dass. I kept abreast of these subjects and tried to give responsive answers.

That all changed. The lecture committee arrived at the airport wearing three piece suits, briefcases, clipboards with schedules. No music. No questions about Michael Jackson's theory of reincarnation or Sheena Easton's concept of sugar walls. The impudent grins were gone. The young people were cool, realistic, and corporate-minded. They questioned me about computer stocks, electronic books, and prospects for careers in software.

Anatomy of a Yuppie

The moralists of both left and right can froth with righteous indignation about this army of selfish, career-oriented, entrepreneurial individualists who apparently value money and their own interests more than the lofty causes of yesteryear. But behind the trendy hype, we sense that the twitchy media may be reflecting some authentic change in the public consciousness.

> **The phrase "young urban professionals" didn't tell us much. I guess the implication was that they were not old rural amateurs— ORAs. But who were they?**

The yuppie myth expressed a vague sense that something different, something not yet understood but possibly meaningful, was happening in the day-to-day lives and dreams of young people growing up in this very unsettling world.

Surely it's important to understand what was going on with this most influential group of human beings on the planet—the 76 million materialistic, educated or streetwise, performance-driven Americans becoming adults in the latter 20th Century.

 ## Yuppies were a new breed

This much we know: The yuppies were a new breed. They were the first members of the electronic society. They were the first crop of bewildered mutants climbing out of the muck of the industrial—late neolithic smokestack—age. They showed up on the scene in 1946, a watershed year, marking the end of World War II—the war that induced the birth of electronic technology: radar, sonar, atomic fission, computers. In 1946, this incredible high-tech gear was beginning to be available for civilian consumption.

Something else important happened in 1946. The birthrate in America unexpectedly doubled. Between 1946 and 1964, 76 million babies were born. That's 40 million more than demographers predicted. These postwar kids were the first members of a new species: *Homo sapiens electronicus.* From the time they could peer out of the crib, they were exposed to a constant shower of information beaming from screens.

They were, right from the start, treated like no other generation in human history. Their parents raised them according to Dr. Benjamin Spock's totally revolutionary theory of child care. "Treat your kids as individuals," said Spock. "Tell them that they are special! Tell them to think for themselves. Feed them, not according to some factory schedule. Feed them on gourmet demand, i.e., let 'em eat what they want when they are hungry."

Postwar kids were the first members of a new species, Homo sapiens electronicus. From the time they could peer out of the crib, they were exposed to a constant shower of information beaming from screens.

This generation is the most intelligent group of human beings ever to inhabit the planet. The best educated. The most widely traveled. The most sophisticated. They have grew up adapting to an accelerated rate of change that is almost incomprehensible. They became highly selective consumers, expecting to be rewarded because they are the best.

Let's hasten to clear up one misconception here. This postwar generation of Spockies was not docilely manipulated by greedy ad men or the cynical media. Nor was it the so called image makers, the rock stars and television programmers and moviemakers, telling the kids what to do. Quite to the contrary. The Spockies themselves dictated to the imageers and marketeers about what they wanted.

Baby-Boomers Grow Up

W The rapidly changing style and tone of American culture in the second half of the 20th Century has reflected the elitist expectations of this Spock generation as it passed through the normal stages of maturation.

During the 1950s, kids were clean cut and easygoing. The tumultuous Sixties marked the stormy adolescence of this astonishing generation and bore the hippies—bands of cheerful, muddling sensualists and self-proclaimed dropouts. By the 1970s, Spockies were busy stopping the Vietnam War, peaceably overthrowing the Nixon administration, and mainly trying to figure out what to do with their lives. The Eighties brought us a new breed of individualists turned professional.

The Fifties are fondly remembered as the child-centered, home-based decade. Popular music, being most free from parental control, provided the clearest expression of youthful mood. The first stirrings of adolescence changed the beat. Spockies wanted to wiggle their hips tentatively; so the hula-hoop craze swept the land. The music picked up the beat with rhythm 'n' blues, rockabilly, rock 'n' roll, the Surfer and the Motown sound. Just as cute, fuzzy caterpillars suddenly metamorphose into gaudy butterflies, so did the sweet, cuddly Mouseketeers moult into high-flying, highly visible, highly vulnerable hippies.

The Spockies emerging into teenage pubescence in the 1960s changed our traditional notions about sex, duty, work, conformity, and sacrifice. The postwar kids never really accepted the values of the industrial society or the aesthetics of the Depression era. They never bought the Protestant work ethic. After watching television six hours a day for fifteen years, would they settle docilely for a hard hat job on the assembly line?

Bob Dylan set the tone for the adolescent rebellion: "Don't follow leaders. Watch your parking meters." The Beach Boys offered a California style of personal freedom. The Beatles picked up the theme of bouncy irreverence. It seemed so natural. All you need is love. Do your own thing.

The Sixties were unflurried, unworried, more erotic than neurotic. We're not gonna be wage slaves or fight the old men's wars. We're all gonna live in a yellow submarine!

It wasn't just middle class white males calling for changes. The blacks were ready. They had been waiting four hundred years. The race riots and the civil-rights protests and the freedom marches were an unexpected fallout of Spockian philosophy. It is hard to overestimate the effect of the black culture on the Spockie generation. There was the music, of course. The style, the grace, the coolness, the cynical Zen detachment from the system came from the blacks. No white professor had to tell the blacks to turn on, tune in, and drop out of conformity.

Then there was the women's liberation movement, perhaps the most significant change impulse of the century. This was the smartest, best-educated group of women in history, and they expected to be treated as individuals. And the gay-pride concept was stirring. Apparently their parents had read Spock, too. Not since the democratic, human-rights movements of the 18th Century had there been so much feverish hope for a fair and free social order.

But by the end of the decade it became apparent that utopia wasn't going to happen that easily.

Why Utopia Isn't Going to Happen

1. There were powerful forces dead-set against any change in American culture.

2. There were no practical blueprints or role models for harnessing a vague philosophy of individualism into a functioning social order.

3. Basically, we were not quite ready: The Spockies were still kids outnumbered demographically and unprepared psychologically to create the postindustrial phase of human culture.

The opposition to change had made itself very apparent in the cold-blooded assassinations of Jack Kennedy, brother Bobby, Malcolm X, and Martin Luther King, Jr. Lyndon Johnson, Richard Nixon, and the new cowboy governor of California made it perfectly clear that they would happily use force to protect their system.

The social philosophy of the hippies was romantically impractical. Sure, they weren't gonna work on Maggie's farm no more, but what were they gonna do after bailing all night long? Some retreated to gurus, others went back to a new form of anti-technological chic Amishness. Urban political activists parroted slogans of European or third-world socialism and made pop stars of totalitarian leaders like Che Guevara and Ho Chi Minh. The debacle at Altamont and the conjunction of overdose deaths of rock stars Joplin, Hendrix, and Morrison symbolized the end of the Sixties.

The Next Phase

By the end of the Sixties, many young people had lost confidence in the old establishments. The phrase "Don't trust anyone over 30" re-flected a disillusioned realism; you couldn't find answers in the grand ol' GOP or the Democratic party. Big business and big labor were both unresponsive to the obvious need for change; the high ideals of socialism seemed to translate into just another word for police-state bureaucracy. By the end of the decade, it was also clear to any sensible young person that individualism and doing your own thing had a certain drawback. If you weren't gonna work for Maggie's pa no more, how were you gonna make out?

The obvious answer: You were gonna believe in yourself. That's what the Seventies were all about. More than 76 mil-lion Spockies reached the venerable age of 24 and faced a very practical challenge: Grow up!

The focus became self-improvement, EST,

> Those who think for themselves—free agents—tend to see computers as thought-appliances.

assertiveness training, personal excellence, career planning. Tom Wolfe, always the shrewd social critic, coined the term "the me generation."

Then a recession hit. Arab-oil blackmail
pushed up inflation rates. Adult society had no
expansion-growth plans to harness the energies
of 40 million extra people. Indeed, growing au-
tomation was reducing the work force. The Iran
hostage crisis lowered morale. In the malaise,
the voters chose the smiling Ronald Reagan over
a frustrated Carter. The Spockies boycotted the
election.

Most young Americans today don't want to be
forced to work at jobs that can be done better by
machines. They don't want to stand on assembly
lines repeating mindless tasks. Robots work. Citizens in socialist workers' countries work. Grizzled
veterans in the steel towns of Pennsylvania work.
Third-world people have to work to survive.

What do self-respecting, intelligent, ambi-
tious young Americans do? They perform. They
master a craft. They learn to excel in a personal
skill. They become entrepreneurs, i.e., people
who organize, operate, and assume risks. They
employ themselves, they train themselves, they
promote themselves, they transfer themselves,
they reward themselves.

They perform exactly those functions that
can't be done by CAD-CAM machines, however
precisely programmed. They gravitate naturally
to postindustrial fields-electronics, communication, education, merchandising, marketing, entertainment, skilled personal service, health and
growth enterprises, leisure-time professions.

They are politically and psychologically independent. They do not identify with company or union or partisan party. They do not depend on organizational tenure. They are notoriously non-loyal to institutions.

Cyberpunks are the inventors,
innovative writers, techno-frontier
artists, risk-taking film directors,
icon-shifting composers, stand-up
comedians, expressionist artists,
free-agent scientists, techno-
creatives, computer visionaries,
elegant hackers, bit-blithng Prolog
adepts, special-effectives, cognitive
dissidents, video wizards, neurological test pilots, media explorers—
all of those who boldly package
and steer ideas out there where no
thoughts have gone before.

13

CYBERPUNKS

Cyber means "pilot."** A "Cyberperson" is one who pilots his/her own life. By definition, the cyberperson is fascinated by navigational information—especially maps, charts, labels, guides, manuals that help pilot one through life. The cyberperson continually searches for theories, models, paradigms, metaphors, images, icons that help chart and define the realities that we inhabit.

"Cybertech" refers to the tools, appliances, and methodologies of knowing and communicating. Linguistics. Philosophy. Semantics. Semiotics. Practical epistemologies. The ontologies of daily life. Words, icons, pencils, printing presses, screens, keyboards, computers, disks.

"Cyberpolitics" introduces the Foucault notions of the use of language and linguistic-tech by the ruling classes in feudal and industrial societies to control children, the uneducated, and the under classes. The words "governor" or "steersman" or "G-man" are used to describe those who manipulate words and communication devices in order to control, to bolster authority—

feudal, management, government—and to discourage innovative thought and free exchange.

Cyberpunks use all available data-input to think for themselves. You know who they are. Every stage of history has produced names and heroic legends for the strong, stubborn, creative individuals who explore some future frontier, collect and bring back new information, and offer to guide the human gene pool to the next stage. Typically, these time mavericks combine bravery, and high curiosity, with super self-esteem. These three characteristics are considered necessary for those engaged in the profession of genetic guide, aka counterculture philosopher.

The classical Olde Westworld model for the cyberpunk is Prometheus, a technological genius who "stole" lire from the Gods and gave it to humanity. Prometheus also taught his gene pool many useful arts and sciences. According to the official version of the legend, he/she was exiled from the gene pool and sentenced to the ultimate torture for these unauthorized transmissions of classified information. In another version of the myth (unauthorized), Prometheus (aka the Pied Piper) uses his/her skills to escape the sinking kinship taking with him/her the cream of the gene pool.

The classical Olde Westworld model for the cyberpunk is Prometheus, a technological genius who "stole" lire from the Gods and gave it to humanity.

The Newe World version of this ancient myth is Quetzalcoatl, God of civilization, high-tech wizard who introduced maize, the calendar, erotic sculpture, flute-playing, the arts, and the sciences. He was driven into exile by the G-man in power, who was called Tezcatlpoca.

Self-assured singularities of the cyberbreed have been called mavericks, ronin, freelancers, independents, self-starters, nonconformists, oddballs, troublemakers, kooks, visionaries, iconoclasts, insurgents, blue-sky thinkers, loners, smart alecks. Before Gorbachev, the Soviets scornfully called them hooligans. Religious organizations have always called them heretics. Bureaucrats call them disloyal dissidents, traitors, or worse. In the old days, even sensible people called them mad.

They have been variously labeled clever, creative, entrepreneurial, imaginative, enterprising, fertile, ingenious, inventive, resourceful, talented, eccentric.

During the tribal, feudal, and industrial-literate phrases of human evolution, the logical survival traits were conformity and dependability. The "good serf" or "vassal" was obedient. The "good worker" or "manager" was reliable. Maverick thinkers were tolerated only at moments when innovation and change were necessary, usually to deal with the local competition.

In the information communication civilization of the 21st Century, creativity and mental excellence will become the ethical norm. The world will be too dynamic, complex, and diversified, too cross-linked by the global immediacies of modern—quantum—communication, for stability of thought or dependability of behavior to be successful. The "good persons" in the cy-

> **Cyberpunks use all available data-input to quesiton authority andthink for themselves**

bernetic society are the intelligent ones who can think for themselves. The "problem person" in the cybernetic society of the 21st Century is the one who automatically obeys, who never, questions authority, who acts to protect his/her official status, who placates and politics rather than thinks independently.

Thoughtful Japanese are worried about the need for ronin thinking in their obedient culture, the postwar generation now taking over.

Greek Word for "Pilot"

The term "cybernetics" comes from the Greek word *kubernetes*, "pilot"

The Hellenic origin of this word is important in that it reflects the Socratic-Platonic traditions of independence and individual self-reliance which, we are told, derived from geography. The proud little Greek city-states were perched on peninsular fingers wiggling down into the fertile Mediterranean Sea, protected by mountains from the land-mass armies of Asia.

Mariners of those ancient days had to be bold and resourceful. Sailing the seven seas without maps or navigational equipment, they were forced to develop independence of thought The self-reliance that these Hellenic pilots developed in their voyages probably carried over to the democratic, inquiring, questioning nature of their land life.

The Athenian cyberpunks, the pilots, made their own navigational decisions.

These psychogeographical factors may have contributed to the humanism of the Hellenic religions that emphasized freedom, pagan joy, celebration of life, and speculative thought. The humanist and polytheistic religions of ancient Greece are often compared with the austere morality of monotheistic Judaism, the fierce, dogmatic polarities of Persian-Arab dogma, and the imperial authority of Roman—Christian—culture.

Roman Concept of Director, Governor, Steersman

The Greek word *kubernetes*, when translated to Latin, comes out as *gubernetes*. This basic verb gubernare means to control the actions or behavior, to direct, to exercise sovereign authority, to regulate, to keep under, to restrain, to steer. This Roman concept is obviously very different from the Hellenic notion of "pilot"

It maybe relevant that the Latin term "to steer" comes from the word stare, which means "to stand," with derivative meanings "place or thing which is standing." The past participle of the Latin word produces "status," "state," "institute," "statue," "static," "statistics," "prostitute," "restitute," "constitute."

The word "cybernetics" was coined in 1948 by Norbert Weiner, who wrote, "we have decided to call the entire field of control and communication theory, whether in the machine or in the animal, by the name of Cybernetics, which we form from the Greek for steersman. [sic]"

The word "cyber" has been redefined in the American Heritage Dictionary as "the theoretical study of control processes in electronic, mechanical, and biological systems, especially the flow of information in such systems." The derivative word "cybernate" means "to control automatically by computer or to be so controlled."

An even more ominous interpretation defines cybernetics as "the study of human control mechanisms and their replacement by mechanical or electronic systems."

Note how Weiner and the Romanesque engineers have corrupted the meaning of "cyber." The Greek word "pilot" becomes "governor" or "director"; the term "to steer" becomes "to control."

Now we are liberating the term, teasing it free from serfdom to represent the autopoetic, self-directed principle of organization that arises in the universe in many systems of widely varying sizes, in people, societies, and atoms.

Politics of Literacy

The etymological distinctions between Greek and Roman terms are quite relevant to the pragmatics of the culture surrounding their usage. French philosophy, for example, has recently stressed the importance of language and semiotics in determining human behavior and social structures. Michel Foucault's classic studies of linguistic politics and mind control led him to believe

that human consciousness—as expressed in speech and images, in self-definition and mutual designation is the authentic locale of the determinant politics of being.... What men and women are born into is only superficially this or that social, legislative, and executive system. Their ambiguous, oppressive birthright is the language, the conceptual categories, the conventions of identification and perception, which have evolved and, very largely, atrophied up to the time of their personal and social existence. It is the established but customarily subconscious, unargued constraints of awareness that enslave.

> To remove the means of expressing dissent is to remove the possibility of dissent.

Orwell and Wittgenstein and McLuhan agree. To remove the means of expressing dissent is to remove the possibility of dissent. "Whereof one cannot speak, thereof must one remain silent." In this light the difference between the Greek word "pilot" and the Roman translation "governor" becomes a most significant semantic manipulation, and the flexibility granted to symbol systems of all kinds by their representation in digital computers becomes dramatically liberating.

Do we pride ourselves for becoming ingenious "pilots" or dutiful "controllers"?

What is Governetics?

The word "governetics" refers to an attitude of obedience-control in relationship to self or others. Pilots, those who navigate on the seven seas or in the sky, have to devise and execute course changes continually in response to the changing environment. They respond continually to feedback, information about the environment. Dynamic. Alert. Alive.

The Latinate "steersman," by contrast, is in the situation of following orders. The Romans, we recall, were great organizers, road-builders, administrators. The galleys, the chariots must be controlled. The legions of soldiers must be directed.

The Hellenic concept of the individual navigating his/her own course was an island of humanism in a raging sea of totalitarian empires. To the East—the past—were the centralized, authoritarian kingdoms. The governors of Iran, from Cyrus, the Persian emperor, to the recent shah and ayatollah, have exemplified the highest traditions of state control.

The Greeks were flanked on the other side, which we shall designate as the West—or future, by a certain heavy concept called Rome. The caesars and popes of the Holy Roman Empire represented the next grand phase of institutional control. The governing hand on the wheel stands for stability, durability, continuity, permanence. Staying the course. Individual creativity, exploration, and change are usually not encouraged.

Pilots of the Species

The terms "cybernetic person" or "cybernaut" return us to the original meaning of "pilot" and puts the self reliant person back in the loop. These words—and the more pop term "cyberpunk"—refer to the personalization—and thus the popularization—of knowledge-information technology, to innovative thinking on the part of the individual.

According to McLuhan and Foucault, if you change the language, you change the society. Following their lead, we suggest that the terms "cybernetic person, cybernaut" may describe a new species model of human being and a new social order. "Cyberpunk" is, admittedly, a risky term. Like all linguistic innovations, it must be used with a tolerant sense of high-tech humor. It's a stopgap, transitional meaning-grenade thrown over the language barricades to describe the resourceful, skillful individual who accesses and steers knowledge-communication technology toward his/her own private goals, for personal pleasure, profit, principle, or growth.

Cyberpunks are the inventors, innovative writers, techno-frontier artists, risk-taking film directors, icon-shifting composers, stand-up comedians, expressionist artists, free-agent scientists, techno-creatives, computer visionaries, elegant hackers, bit-blithng Prolog adepts, special-effectives, cognitive dissidents, video wizards, neurological test pilots, media explorers—all of those who boldly package and steer ideas out there where no thoughts have gone before.

Countercultures are sometimes tolerated by the governors. They can, with sweet cynicism and patient humor, in-

This free-speech/free-thought movement emerges routinely when enough young people have access to electronic technology.

terface their singularity with institutions. They often work within the "governing systems" on a temporary basis. As often as not, they are unauthorized.

The "good persons" in the cybernetic society are the intelligent ones who think for themselves. The "problem persons" in the cybernetic society of the 21st Century are those who automatically obey, who never question authority, who act to protect their official status, who placate and politic rather than thinking independently.

Legend of the Ronin

Ronin is used by Beverly Potter as a metaphor based on a Japanese word for lordless samurai. As early as the 8th Century, ronin was translated literally as "wave people" and used in Japan to describe those who had left their allotted, caste-predetermined stations in life: samurai who left the service of their feudal lords to become masterless.

Ronin played a key role in Japan's abrupt transition from a feudal society to industrialism. Under feudal rule, warriors were not allowed to think freely, or act according to their will. On the other hand, having been forced by circumstances to develop independence, ronin took more readily to new ideas and technology and became increasingly influential in the independent schools.

—Beverly Potter
The Way of the Ronin

The West has many historical parallels to the ronin archetype. The term "free lance" has its origin in the period after the Crusades, when a large number of knights were separated from their lords. Many lived by the code of chivalry and became "lances for hire." The American frontier was fertile ground for the ronin archetype. "Maverick," derived from the Texan word for unbranded steer, was used to describe a free and self-directed individual.

Although many of the ronin's roots ... are in the male culture, most career women are well acquainted with the way of the ronin. Career women left their traditional stations and battled their way into the recesses of the male dominated workplaces.... Like the ronin who had no clan, professional women often feel excluded from the corporate cliques' inside tracks, without ally or mentor.

—Beverly Potter
The Way of the Ronin

Role Model for 21st Century

The tradition of the "individual who thinks for him/herself" extends to the beginnings of recorded human history. Indeed, the very label of our species, Homo sapiens, defines us as the animal who thinks.

If our genetic function is computare—to think, then it follows that the ages and stages of human history, so far, have been larval or preparatory. After the insectoid phases of submission to gene pools, the mature stage of the human life cycle is the individual who thinks for him/herself. Now at the beginnings of the information age, are we ready to assume our genetic function?

The beats stood for the ecstatic vision and for individual freedom in revolt against all bureaucratic, closed-minded systems. They saw themselves as citizens of the world. They met with Russian poets to denounce the Cold War. They practiced oriental yoga. They experimented, as artists have for centuries, with mind-opening foods and drugs and sexual practices.

14

A NEW BREED

I t had finally happened: the inevitable and long-awaited climax of the youth revolutions. "They aren't going to work on Brezhnev's farm no more." The Dr. Spock-memes of self-direction has swept the world in less than three decades.

This is not a political revolution; it's more like a cultural evolution. A tsunami of electronic information. The emergence of a new breed. Young people all over the world are mutated, as Marshall McLuhan predicted, by highly communicable memes: documentary footage, rock 'n' roll music, MTV pirate broadcasts, all coming to them through American-Japanese television screens. This new breed is centered on self-direction and individual choice, a genetic revulsion for partisan politics, a species horror of centralized governments.

This global youth movement cannot be discussed in the terms of politics or sociology or psychology. We are dealing with a new, post-Darwinian, genetic science.

This emergence of youth power has been called sociogenetics, cybernetic evolution, cultural genetics, memetics. It has to do with the communication and transmission of new ideas and attitudes. Dawkins has suggested the word "memes" to describe these self-replicating ideas that sweep across human populations, bringing about cultural mutations.

Memes: Self-replicating ideas that sweep across human populations, bringing about cultural mutations.

Neoteny: (1) attainment of improved functional maturity during the larval stage; (2) retention of survivally optimal larval or immature characters as adults, i.e., refusal to stop growing, extension of the developmental period.

At the end of the 20th Century, we witnessed a new breed emerging during the juvenile stage of industrial-age society. The key word here is juvenile, as opposed to adult. Adult is the past participle of the verb "to grow." This new breed appeared when enormous numbers of individuals in the juvenile stage began intercommunicating some new memes, mutating together at the same time. The Japanese brand of this youth movement call themselves Ho Ko Ten—"the new society."

Biological evolution works through the competitive spread of genes. Logically, the mechanism of cultural change involves communication.

Individuals are activated to change when they pick up new meme-signals from others of their cohort The mode of communication determines not just the speed of the change, but the nature of the change.

Medium is the Message in the Cultural Evolution

The Ten Commandments, chiseled on stone tablets, created a fundamentalist culture that discouraged change and democratic participation. There is one God, the author-creator, and his words are eternally true. This stone—tablet meme—carrier spawns a culture ruled by the inerrant "good book" and a priest-hood of those who preserve, interpret, and en-force the commandments.

The printing press mass-disseminates memes that create a factory culture run by managers.

The electronic, McLuhanesque meme-signals that produced Woodstock nation and the Berlin Wall deconstruction are more a matter of atti-tude and style.

The television news has trained us to rec-ognize "the robe-memes"— the feudal pope—or Iranian mullah—and his solemn piety-reek-ing priests. We recognize "the suits", the adult politicians of the industrial age, with their no-nonsense sobriety. We observe "the uniforms", armed, booted, helmeted.

And since the Sixties, we have observed this new breed, "the students" who tend to wear blue jeans and running shoes. Their dress and ges-tural signals are as important as the identify-

ing markings and scents of different species of
mammals. Just like any new breed of mammals,
these kids recognize each other across national
boundaries. The faces of the Chinese youth shine
with that same glow as the faces photographical-
ly captured in Berlin and Prague and—twenty
years previously—in Woodstock.

Prime-Time Authoritarianism

It is important to note that these students are
not demonstrating for "socialist democracy" or
"capitalist democracy." They are for "individual
freedom". In the cybernetic age, "democracy"
becomes majority-mob rule and the enemy of
individual freedom.

Democracy works just fine in a preindustrial,
oral society in which the men walk or ride horses
to the village center and talk things over. Industrial societies produce a factory system of politics
run by managers. Representative government involves full-time professional politicians and partisan parties. The dismal results are predictable.

As soon as cybernetic communication appliances emerged, political power was seized by
those who control the airwaves. We've seen this
since the rise of fascism and totalitarianism.
American elections in the Eighties produced an
ominous demonstration of tele-democracy in a
centralized country.

Less than 50 percent of the eligible voters both-
ered to register or vote in these three presidential
elections. More than half of adult Americans were
so disillusioned, apathetic, bored that they made

the intelligent decision to vote, in absentia, for "none of the above." According to exit polls, more than half of voting Americans glumly admitted that they were choosing "the lesser of two evils."

Republican presidents in the Eighties were elected by around 25 percent of the citizenry. The only ones who really cared about these elections were those who stood to benefit financially from the results. The "apparatchiks" and government-payrolled "nomenclatura" of the two contending "parties" choose the "leaders" who would preside over division of the spoils.

History will note that the Eighties Republican mirrored the Brezhnevian anomie in the Soviet Union. It is now shockingly clear that the Republican party in this country plays the role of the Communist party in the pre-Gorbachev USSR: an entrenched, conservative, militaristic, unashamedly corrupt, secretive, belligerently nationalistic bureaucracy. It gave the country twelve years of stagnation, spiritless boredom, and cynical greed.

Meanwhile, the all-star huckster of freedom and decentralization, Mikhail Gorbachev, in five remarkable years persuaded an entire subcontinent to "drop out" of Stalinism.

In this climate it is obvious that the party apparatus with the biggest budget for television advertising and the marketing ability to focus on the most telegenic, shallow, flamboyantly lurid issues (abortion, drugs, pledge of allegiance, school prayer, no taxes, and jingoistic, bellicose nationalism) would sweep to a landslide win on the votes of the 25 percent majority.

> **This new breed is centered on self-direction and individual choice, a genetic revulsion for partisan politics, a species horror of centralized governments.**

It is ironic that in the oldest democracy, the U.S., partisan politics seems to have lost touch with reality. In the elections of the Eighties, millions were expended on political advertising. Elections were won by paid-time commercials involving moralistic images, emotional theatrics, and malicious fabrications. Old-fashioned religious demonology and fake patriotism, skillfully splashed across the television screens, replaced rational discussion of issues.

End of Majoritarian Democracy

In the feudal and industrial ages, majoritarian democracy was usually a powerful libertarian counterculture force defending the individual against regal tyranny and class slavery. In the early years of the electronic-information stage (1950-1990), the ability of the religious-industrial-military rulers to manipulate television converted town hall democracy into majoritarian, prime-time, sit-corn totalitarianism.

Cybernetic media in the hands of politicians with shockingly large advertising budgets plays to the dread LCD—lowest common denominator. The new fragile democracies in eastern Europe will probably have to pass through this phase of marketeer, televoid elections manipulated by "spin doctors" and dishonest advertising.

So much for the down side. The good news is that cybernetic media cannot be controlled. Electronic signals flashing around the atmosphere cannot be kept out by stone walls or border police dogs. Japanese tape-decks, ghetto-blasters, digital appliances in the hands of the individual empowers the HCD—highest common denominator.

Sociology of Quantum Physics

The philosophy that predicted this movement is not capitalism or socialism. It is not industrial democracy—the tyranny of the 25 percent majority. Psychedelic concepts like glasnost and perestroika are based on the common-sense principles of quantum physics—relativity, flexibility, singularity.

Werner Heisenberg's equations described the fabrication of singular, personal realities based on free, open communication. Objective indeterminacy, that bane of the mechanical mind, means individual determinism and self-reliance—the mottoes of the new breed.

Dr. Spock Personalizes Quantum Psychology

In 1946, quantum physics was translated into common-sense, hands-on psychology by a pediatrician. The youth movement was generated by a genial child psychologist who taught two generations of postwar parents to feed their children on demand. "Treat your kids as individuals, as singularities." Here was the most radical, subversive social doctrine ever proposed, and it was directed to the only groups that can bring about enduring change: parents, pediatricians, teachers.

This postwar generation of indulged, "self-centered" individuals started to appear exactly when the new psychedelic-cybernetic brain change technologies became available to individuals.

McLuhan Empowers Quantum Psychology

The babyboomers were the first television species, the first human beings who used electronic digital appliances to turn on and tune in realities; the first to use neurotransmitting chemicals to change their own brains; the first members of this "global village" made possible by television.

The fall of the Berlin Wall was accomplished by youth seeking individual freedom. This student counterculture started in America in the 1960s, and it was spread via electronic media.

"Hongk is all the rage in the Mongolian People's Republic. It's a key part of the Shineshiel (perestroika) that has been sweeping the remote communist nation for weeks now.... Hongk is the name of the rock 'n' roll band that has been playing its powerful, dissident songs to packed audiences in the state owned auditoriums of Mongolia's capitol of Ulan Bator for months now. Its music has become the unchallenged anthem of the city's fledgling protest movement" (*Los Angeles Times*).

Function of Post-Democratic Government

The primary function of a free society in the post-democratic age is the protection of individual freedom from politicians who attempt to limit personal freedom.

This individual-freedom movement is new to human history, because it is not based on geography, politics, class, or religion. It has to do with changes, not in the power structure, not in who controls the police, but in the individual's mind. It is a "head" revolution: a consciousness-raising affair. It involves "thinking for yourself." This cultural meme involves intelligence, personal access to information, an anti-ideological reliance on common sense, mental proficiency, consciousness raising, street smarts, intelligent consumerism-hedonism, personal-communication skills. The meme-idea is not new. Counter-cultures go back at least as far as Hermes Trismegistus, and include Socrates, Paracelsus, the Renaissance, Voltaire, Emerson, Thoreau, Dada, Gurdjieff, and Crowley.

But the rapid spread of this mutational meme from 1960 to 1990 was due to the sudden, mass availability of neurochemical and electronic technology. Demand feeding. Chemicals and screens spraying electronic information into eye drums and ear balls, activating brains. Suddenly, youth all over the world are wearing jeans and listening to John Lennon's "Give Peace a Chance." The individuality meme that swept American youth during the Sixties has infected the world.

J.F.K. was a memetic agent, literally creating a new breed!

In the Seventies, the Spock-McLuhan epidemic spread around western Europe. The signs

of this awakening are always the same. Young
minds exposed to the free spray of electronic
information suddenly blossom like flowers in the
spring. The June 1989 demonstrations in Tien
An Men square were a classic replay of Chicago
1968 and Kent State 1970.

Power, Mao said, comes from the barrel of a
gun. That may have been true in the industrial
past, but in cybernetic Ninties, the very notion
of political "power" seems anachronistic, kinky,
sick. For the new breed the notion of "political
power" is hateful, evil, ghastly. The idea that any
group should want to grab domination, control,
authority, supremacy, or jurisdiction over others is a primitive perversity—as loathsome and
outdated as slavery or cannibalism.

It was not the Berlin Wall of concrete and
guard houses that protected the "evil empire"; it
was the electronic wall that was easily breached
by MTV. McLuhan and Foucault have demonstrated that freedom depends upon who controls
the technologies that reach your brain-tele-
phones, the editing facility, the neurochemicals,
the screen.

Mass Individualism is New

This sudden emergence of humanism
and open-mindedness on a mass scale
is new.

In tribal societies the role of the individual
is to be a submissive, obedient child. The tribal
elders do the thinking. Survival pressures do not
afford them the luxury of freedom.

In feudal societ-
ies the individual is
a serf or vassal, peas-
ant, chattel, peon,
slave. The nobles and
priests do the thinking.
They are trained by
tradition to abhor and
anathematize open mindedness and thinking for
yourself.

This sudden emergence of humanism and open-mindedness on a mass scale is new.

After the tribal—familial—arid feudal—
childlike—stages of human evolution came the
industrial—insectoid—society, where the individual is a worker or manager, in later stages, a
worker-consumer.

In all these static, primitive societies, the
thinking is done by the organizations who control the guns. The power of open-minded individuals to make and remake decisions about their
own lives, to fabricate, concoct, invent, prevari-
cate their own lies is severely limited. Youth had
no power, no voice, no choice.

The post-political information society; which
we are now developing, does not operate on the
basis of obedience and conformity to dogma. It
is based on individual thinking, scientific know-
how, quick exchange of facts around feedback
networks, high tech ingenuity, and practical,
front-line creativity. The society of the future no
longer grudgingly tolerates a few open minded
innovators. The cybernetic society is totally
dependent on a large pool of such people, communicating at light speed with each other across
state lines and national boundaries. Electrified

> **The postwar generation of indulged, "self-centered" individuals appeared when the new psychedelic-cybernetic brain change technologies became available to individuals.**

thoughts invite fast feedback, creating new global societies that require a higher level of electronic know how, psychological sophistication, and open minded intelligence.

This cyber communication process is accelerating so rapidly that to compete on the world information market of the 21st Century, nations, companies, even families must be composed of change-oriented, innovative individuals who are adepts in communicating via the new cyber electronic technologies.

The new breeds are simply much smarter than the old guard. They inhale new information the way they breathe oxygen. They stimulate each other to continually upgrade and reformat their minds. People who use cyber technology to make fast decisions on their jobs are not going to go home and passively let aging, closed-minded white, male politicians make decisions about their lives.

The emergence of this new open-minded caste in different countries around the world is the central historical issue of the last fifty years.

The Revolutions Began with the Beats

In the Fifties in America, at the height of the television Cold War, there appeared a group of free people who created highly communicable counterculture memes that were to change history. The beats stood for the ecstatic vision and for individual freedom in revolt against all bureaucratic, dosed minded systems. They saw themselves as citizens of the world. They met with Russian poets to denounce the Cold War. They practiced oriental yoga. They experimented, as artists have for centuries, with mind opening foods and drugs and sexual practices.

Most important, with their minds turning like satellite dishes to other cultures, they had an historical sense of what they were doing. They saw themselves as heirs to the long tradition of intellectual and artistic individualism that goes beyond national boundaries.

What made the beats more effective than any dissident-artist group in human history was the timing. Electronic technology made it possible for their bohemian memes, their images, and their sounds to be broadcast at almost the speed of light around the world. Just as soap companies were using television and radio to market their products, so the beats used the electronic media to advertise their ideas. The hippie culture of the Sixties and the liberation movements in Eastern Europe are indebted to the libertarian dissenting of the 'fifties counterculture.

Bringing the Sixties to China

The Be-In in San Francisco in January of 1967 produced an ocean of youth who gathered to celebrate their beings and their solidarity. It turned out to be the dawning of the psychedelic-cybernetic age—or glasnost, as it is now called. The San Francisco Be-In was

not organized. The word got out via the underground press, progressive radio stations, word
of mouth. Three months later the International
Monterey Pop festival harnessed the flourishing
psychedelic spirit to electrically amplified music.

The symbol of the counterculture was the
widely repeated image of a young man putting a
flower in the gun barrel of the National Guards-
man who was threatening him. The students in
Tien An Men Square in June 1989 remembered.
Their stated purpose was to bring the Sixties to
China. The epidemic of freedom-memes in China
caught the authorities totally off guard—just
like the numbers at the Woodstock festival.

Self-Government

Partisan politics is over. In the post-political age,
people are catching on to the bottom-line fact: The
only function of a political party is to keep itself in office.

This free-speech/free-thought movement
emerges routinely when enough young people
have access to electronic technology. When the
rulers of China made telephones and television
sets available to millions of people, the swarming of activated youth in Tien An Men Square
was guaranteed. Many of the Chinese students
had seen television coverage of student demonstrations in other countries. When East German
television stations began transmitting programs
from the West, the Berlin Wall was on its way
down. In each nation, the free-thought movement of the Eighties was produced by students
and intellectuals who learned how to use electronic
appliances and digital computers to think for

themselves, fabricate their personal mythologies, and communicate their irreverent aspirations.

Politics of Choice

Freedom is an individual thing. It means something singular, unique, personal for each and every person. The Chinese students want something that is not mentioned by Marx or Margaret Thatcher. They want to say what's on their minds. The right to make their own career decisions. The right to choose their college major. The right to be silly and have fun. The right to kiss your boyfriend in public. The right to mug in front of a television camera. The right to flaunt their own personal lies, concoctions, invented truths in competition with the old official lies.

Gorbachev was dismayed to find that many Soviet youth, given freedom of the press, were more interested in UFOs, punk rock, astrology, and hashish than in political issues.

Designer Memes

Most young people in the liberated lands want to de-politicize, demili-tarize, decentral-ize, secularize, and globalize.

The new breed is jumping the gene pools, form-ing post-industri-

The pop term "turn on" carries the fascinating cybernetic implication that one can selectively dial up or access brain sectors that process specific channels of information signals normally unavailable.

al, global meme-pools. They are the informates. From their earliest years, most of their defining memes came flashing at light speed across borders in digital-electronic form, light signals received by screens and radios and record players. Their habitat is the electron sphere, the environment of digital signals that is called the info world. The global village.

They are the first generation of our species to discover and explore Cyberia. They are migrating not to a new place, but to a wide open new time. The new breed is fashioning, conceiving, and designing the realities we will inhabit.

Designer Societies of the 21st Century

Who controls the screen controls the mind of the screen watcher. The power-control struggles of the early 21st Century will occur on screens in the living rooms of individuals.

In nations where religious or partisan political groups control the screens to fabricate paranoias, the people will be incited to fear, anger, and moral outrage. At the dawn of the 21st Century, the Islamic states and the USA under Republican administration effectively made this point.

The manufacture and distribution of inexpensive communications appliances and software is of enormous importance. Just as the USSR and the USA controlled the world for forty years by distributing weapons to every compliant dictatorship, Japanese and Silicon Valley companies are liberating the world with an endless flood of electronic devices designed for individuals.

The social and political implications of this democratization of the screen are enormous. In the past, friendship and intimate exchange were limited to local geography or occasional visits. Now you can play electronic tennis with a pro in Tokyo, interact with a classroom in Paris, cyberflirt with cute guys in

Who controls the screen controls the mind of the screen watcher.

any four cities of your choice. A global fast-feedback language of icons and memes, facilitated by instant translation devices, smoothly eliminates the barriers of language that have been responsible for most of the war and conflict of the last centuries.

Inexpensive appliances allow individuals to write on their screens the way Gutenberg hardware-software allowed individuals to write on pages five hundred years ago. These inexpensive digitizing and editing devices are transforming the home into a cyberstudio in which individuals design, edit, perform, and transmit memes on their screens.

Individuals clothed in cyberwear will be able to meet each other in virtual realities built for two. The world becomes a neighborhood in which a person eight thousand miles away can be "right there in your windowpane."

15

CYBER CULTURES

This impassioned rhetoric was the first time that the leader of a superpower or empire had ever used the powerful meme: "generation." J.F.K. was a memetic agent, literally creating a new breed!

Did the speech writers who in 1960 passed along to Jack Kennedy that famous "torch" quote intuit what was going to happen? Did they foresee that the next two decades would produce, for the first time in human history, an economic, political power base called "the youth culture"?

In the Fifties, this new baby-boom generation was tuning in the dials of a new electronic-reality appliance called television to Leave It to Beaver and American Bandstand. And they were being lovingly guarded in maximum-security homes by devoted parents who had dutifully memorized Dr. Benjamin Spock's *Common-Sense Guide to Child Care.*

The basic theme of Spock's manual—we parents actually called it the Bible—is: treat your children as individuals.

This innocent bombshell exploded at a pregnant moment of postwar national prosperity and global self-confidence, The Marshall Plan was pouring billions into the rehabilitation-recovery of former enemies. Instead of looting, raping, and occupying the defeated enemies, we treated them like errant offspring who had become delinquent gang members. We helped them get on their feet again and gain self-respect. We postwar Spock parents became the first generation to honor and respect our children and to support their independence from us.

The importance of this event is hard to overestimate. The baby-boomers became the first generation of electronic consumers. Before they were ten, their brains were processing more "realities per day" than their grandparents had confronted in a year.

Parental Home Media

In 1950, the humble black-and-white television set marked the birth of the electronic culture. Suddenly, humans had developed electronic technology and the know-how to operate the brain and reprogram the mind.

The neurological situation is this: The language circuits of the brain are imprinted between ages three and eight. The media used in the home will format the brain of these children. Linguist-psychologists, like Noman Chomsky, and Piaget, demonstrated that languages are imprinted during this brief window of imprint vulnerability. This means that the home media used by the family formats the thought-process-

> **The language circuits of the brain are imprinted between ages three and eight. The media used in the home will format the brain of these children.... If the parents do not read and if there are no newspapers, magazines, or books in the house, the kids are at a tremendous disadvantage.**

ing files—left-brain mind—of the children. Mind-change—reformatting—could occur only under conditions that duplicate "the home culture."

If the parents do not read and if there are no newspapers, magazines, or books in the house, the kids are at a tremendous disadvantage when they timidly walk—or swagger—into the scary, impersonal first grade classroom. Most good teachers understand this principle, and convert the schoolroom into a homey, supportive environment.

We also sense the implications for reformatting mind-files—formerly known as remedial reading. Cultures or individuals who wish to change must use different language media. For the illiterate, delinquent gang member, we offer a maximum-security, homelike environment jammed with media coaches. Malcolm X, for example, was taught to read by a stern, loving parent figure in a Massachusetts prison.

And the rest you oughta know!

Stages of Humanization

As I flash back on my seventy-six years of service as Self-Appointed Change Agent and Evolutionary Scout, this viewpoint comes into focus. Our species has, in seven decades, surfed bigger, faster, more complex waves of brain change than our species experienced during the last 25,000 years.

Number of tribal generations from cave-wall painting to hand-writing and large-scale, public Egyptian art (3200 B.C.)?
➬ About 1,500.

Number of feudal generations from the pyramids to Notre Dame Cathedral, oil painting, and book literacy?
➬ About 320.

Number of generations from first factory-printed book—the first home media—to the radios, telephones, record players, movies of A.D. 1950?
➬ About 23

Number of generations from passive, black-and-white television in 1950 to multi-channel, multimedia, interactive digital home-screen design? ➬ 3

If you change the language, you change the society.

Generational Thing

Each generation since 1950 is the equivalent of an age or an epic or an era in past history. Each succeeding generation has accessed more-powerful electronic-language tools. For the first time, we can understand the mechanics of evolution the language and technology. Finally, the evolution of human brain power is reaching the optimum mutation rate. Electronic brain tools change so rapidly that every fifteen to twenty years the new generation creates a new breed.

Each stage of human culture defines memetic evolution in terms of its media, its language. And the media and languages of cultures determine whether they actively evolve or if they remain passive and unchanging.

Static cultures have built-in, iron-clad linguistic protections against change. Their media-languages self-replicate via repetition, rote-learning, etc. Their reproductive media.

Languages glorify death as the step to eternal life in well-advertised, perfectly run retirement communities called Heaven, etc. Their media-languages prevent them from being exposed to, infected by, or fertilized by other languages.

> In seven decades, humans surfed bigger, faster, more complex waves of brain change than our species experienced during the last 25,000 years.

To illustrate the importance of language in cultural solidarity, we cite the case of the Iranian Shi'ite ayatollahs who put a $5 million price "on the head" of author Salman Rushdie for a few taboo words in a novel published in far away England. Or the case of militant Christians who try to force tax supported schools to teach biblical creationism.

Cultures Evolve Only When Their Media Languages Have Built-In Programs:

1. To discourage rote self-replication;

2. To stimulate self-change via shock-humor, irreverent counterculture, chaotics, etc.;

3. To invite fusion with other cultures, and fusion with other media-languages.

Feudal languages gave no words or graphics that encouraged, tolerated, or even mentioned the notion of evolution during earthly life. The almighty male God creates and controls. Heaven is the destination. Chaos, complexity, change are demonized, tabooed.

Inexpensive appliances will allow individuals to write on their screens the way Gutenberg hardware-software allowed individuals to write on pages five hundred years ago.

The tech-mech engineers of the industrial age—1500-1950—published texts, manuals, and handbooks defining evolution in terms of a Newtonian-Darwinian-Gordon Liddy competitive power struggle: survival of the most brutal, and by the book.

The Information Age

In the information age, evolution is defined in terms of brain power.

- The ability to operate the brain: activate, boot up, turn on, access neurochannels.

- The ability to reformat and re-edit mind-files.

- The ability to receive, process, send messages at light speed.

- The ability to communicate in the multimedia mode; to invent audiographic dictionaries and audiographic grammars.

The mainstream home-media array of inexpensive multimedia appliances has combined the computer, television, video-cassette recorder, fax, compact-disc player, telephone, etc., into one personal home-digital system. During the feudal culture, brain power changed little from century to century. In the mechanical culture, media machines like telephone and radio reached Main Street homes a few decades after their inven-

The post-political information society, which we are now developing, does not operate on the basis of obedience and conformity to dogma. It is based on individual thinking, scientific know-how, quick exchange of facts around feedback networks, high-tech ingenuity, and practical, front-line creativity. The society of the future no longer grudgingly tolerates a few open-minded innovators. The cybernetic society is totally dependent on a large pool of such people, communicating at light speed with each other across state lines and national boundaries.

tion. But the explosion of brain power in the electronic culture in the second half of the 20th Century requires precise birth dates for each generation.

Light Cultures and Countercultures

As brain power accelerates exponentially, we can locate with precision the birth dates of the post-mech cultures.

Americans who were ages three to eight around 1950 became the first primitive electronic culture. As kids, they sat in front of the television and learned how to turn on, tune in, and turn off. Let us call them the "Ike-Knows-Best-Leave-It-to-Beavers," whose parents were sometimes known by the term "conformist."

They were happy. But they were not hip. Their bland passivity instigated the perfect antidote—the counterculture, which initially appears during the sociosexual imprint window known as adolescence.

The Beats! Hipsters! Rebels! They smoked weed and scored junk. They despised television. They were shockingly literate. They wrote breakthrough poetry and poetic prose, honored jazz by ultra hip African Americans. They were sexually experimental.

It is useful to see that the beats were older than the Beavers. In the Forties, when the beats were three to eight years old, their home media were radio, films, records, books. The baby-boomers—76 million strong—were the television-watching Beavers of the Fifties and evolved into the hippies of the Sixties. Affluent, self-confident, spoiled consumers, ready to use their television radio skills to be imprinted by turning on Bob Dylan, timing in the Beatles, turning off parent songs, and fine-tuning color screens.

The Nintendo generation of the Eighties became a pioneer group of cybernauts. They were the first humans to zap through the Alice Window and change electronic patterns on the other side of the screen. They will operate in cyberspace, the electronic environment of the 21st Century.

Coming Chaos

The next couple of decades will accelerate this dizzy explosion of brain power. The fragmenting remnants of the old centralized social systems of the feudal and industrial civilizations are crumbling down.

The 21st Century will witness a new global culture, peopled by new breeds who honor human individuality, human complexity, and human potential, enlightened immortals who communicate at light speed and design the technologies for their scientific re-animation.

16

FUTURE LOOK

If one were asked to predict the next stage of human evolution, practical common sense suggests selecting the identifying survival characteristic of our species, what are our survival assets?

The instant glib answer would be that our species is defined by our enormous brains. Our survival asset is not hive intelligence, as in the social insects, but individual intelligence. Our species is classified as *Homo sapiens sapiens.* Victorian scholars apparently decided that we are the creatures who "think about thinking." Our growth as a species centers on our ability to think and communicate. Predictions about our future would focus on improvements in the way we think

Our young, rookie species has recently passed through several stages of intelligence:

1. Tribal: For at least 22,000 years—approximately 25,000 to 3000 B.C.—the technolo-

gies for sapient thinking—communicating were those of a five year old child: bodily, i.e., oral-gestural.

2. Feudal: During an exciting period of approximately 3,350 years—3000 B.C. to A.D. 350—humans living north of the 35th-parallel latitude developed organized feudal agricultural societies. The technologies for thinking-communicating were hand-tooled statues, temples, monuments. Their philosophy was enforced by emperors, caliphs, and kings.

3. It took approximately 1,250 years—A.D. 350 to 1600—to co-opt the feudal kings and to establish the mechanical assembly-line managerial society. In this age, the technologies of thought communication were mechanical printing presses, typewriters, telephones, produced by efficient workers in highly organized factories, run by centralized bureaucracies.

These days most people in the industrial sectors are extremely dependent on digital thoughts and light images presented on screens. The average American

The baby-boomers were the first generation of electronic consumers. Before they were ten, their brains were processing more "realities per day" than their grandparents had confronted in a year.

household watches television 7.4 hours a day. Almost all business transactions are run by software programs communicated on screens. Without conscious choice or fanfare we have migrated from the "real worlds" of voice, hand, machine into the digitized info-worlds variously called hyperspace, cyberspace, or digital physics.

This migration across the screen into the digital info-world marks the first phase of the postindustrial society.

By the end of the first decade in the 21st Century, most humans living in post-industrial habitats will be spending as much time "jacked in" to info-worlds on the other side of the screen as they spend in the material worlds. We will spend seven hours a day actively navigating, exploring, colonizing, exploiting the oceans and continents of digital data. Interscreening—creating mutual digital-realities—will be the most popular and growthful form of human communication.

Interscreening does not imply a derogation or neglect of flesh interactions. Intimacy at the digital level programs and enriches exchanges in the warm levels. You do not lessen the richness of your murmur-touch-contact with your lover because you can also communicate by phone, fax, and hand-scrawled notes. Warm-breath interactions with your touch friends will be more elegant and pleasant with the digital-reality option added.

Interscreening does not imply a derogation or neglect of flesh interactions. Intimacy at the digital level programs and enriches exchanges in the warm levels. You do not lessen the richness of your murmur-touch-contact with your lover because you can also communicate by phone, fax, and hand-scrawled notes. Warm-breath interactions with your touch friends will be more elegant and pleasant with the digital-reality option added.

Future Global Business Will Take Two Directions

- Cybernetic—management of the left
  brain: Mapping and colonizing the
  digital data-worlds located on the
  other side of screens. Interpersonal
  computing. Interscreening with others.
  Building communal info-structures.
  Protecting cyber-spaces from invasion
  and exploitation by others.

- Psybernetic—management of the right
  brain: Mapping and colonizing the
  next frontier—one's own brain. Constructing info environments in one's
  own neuroworld. Linking one's neu-
  rospace to others. Marketing, leasing,
  sharing one's brain power with others.
  Protecting one's brain from invasion
  and exploitation from without.

Digital business will be run by multinational
corporations based in Japan and Switzerland. The
"multinates" will use individual brains as tools.
Just as slaves, serfs, and prostitutes were forced to
lease their bodies during the three predigital stages, people in the early 21st Century will be leasing
their brains. Work will hardly exist. Most physical
tasks will be performed by automated machines.
Body work will be considered a primitive form of
slavery. No human will be forced by economic-po-
litical pressure to perform muscular-mechanical
tasks that can be done better by robots.

In the 21st Century, the old Judo-Christian-Moslem sects will still be around, but they will have little power beyond entertainment and amusement. The future global religion will be intelligence increase. Upgrading rpms. The two main functions of a human being are consumption and production of thought. Our genetic assignment is the receiving, processing, and producing of digital information.

If you think like a bureaucrat, a functionary, a manager, an unquestioning member of a large organization, or a chess player, beware:

You may soon be out-thought!

The Personal Computer was invented by two bearded, long-haired guys, St. Stephen the Greater and St. Steven the Lesser. And to complete the biblical metaphor, the infant prodigy was named after the Fruit of the Tree of Knowledge: the Apple! The controlled substance with which Eve committed the first original sin: Thinking for Herself!

17

A CYBERPUNK MANIFESTO

by Christian A. Kirtchev

We are the **Electronic Minds**, a group of free-minded rebels. Cyberpunks. We live in Cyberspace, we are everywhere, we know no boundaries. This is our manifest. The Cyberpunks' manifest.

I. Cyberpunk

1. We are those, the Different. Technological rats, swimming in the ocean of information.

2. We are the retiring, little kid at school, sitting at the last desk, in the corner of the class room.

3. We are the teenager everybody considers strange.

4. We are the student hacking computer systems, exploring the depth of his reach.

5. We are the grown-up in the park, sitting on a bench, laptop on his knees, programming the last virtual reality.

6. Ours is the garage, stuffed with electronics. The soldering iron in the corner of the desk and the nearby disassembled radio—they are also ours. Ours is the cellar with computers, buzzing printers and beeping modems.

7. We are those who see reality in a different way. Our point of view shows more than ordinary people can see. They see only what is outside, but we see what is inside. That's what we are—realists with the glasses of dreamers.

8. We are those strange people, almost unknown to the neighborhood. People, indulged in their own thoughts, sitting day after day before the computer, ransacking the net for something. We are not often out of home, just from time to time, only to go to the nearby radio shack, or to the usual bar to meet some of the few friends we have, or to meet a client, or to the backstreet druggist—or just for a little walk.

9. We do not have many friends, only a few with whom we go to parties. Everybody else we know we know on the net. Our real friends are there, on the other side of the line. We know them from our favorite IRC channel, from the News-Groups, from the systems we hang-around.

10. We are those who don't give a shit about what people think about us, we don't care what we look like or what people say about us in our absence.

11. The majority of us like to live in hiding, being unknown to everybody except those few we must inevitably have contact with.

12. Others love publicity, they love fame. They are all known in the underground world. Their names are often heard there. But we are all united by one thing—we are Cyberpunks.

13. Society does not understand us, we are "weird" and "crazy" people in the eyes of the ordinary people who live far from information and free ideas. Society denies our way of thinking—a society, living, thinking and breathing in one and only one way—a cliché.

14. They deny us for we think like free people, and free thinking is forbidden.

15. The Cyberpunk has outer appearance, he is no motion. Cyberpunks are people, starting from the ordinary and known to nobody person, to the artist-technomaniac, to the musician, playing electronic music, to the superficial scholar.

16. The Cyberpunk is no literature genre anymore, not even an ordinary subculture. The Cyberpunk is a stand-alone new culture, offspring of the new age. A culture that unites our common interests and views. We are a unit. We are Cyberpunks.

II. Society

1. The Society which surrounds us is clogged with conservancy pulling everything and everybody to itself, while it sinks slowly in the quicksands of time.

2. However doggedly some refuse to believe it, it is obvious that we live in a sick society. The so-called reforms which our governments so adeptly use to boast, are nothing else but a little step forward, when a whole jump can be done.

3. People fear the new and unknown. They prefer the old, the known and checked truths. They are afraid of what the new can bring to them. They are afraid that they can lose what they have.

4. Their fear is so strong that it has pro-
   claimed the revolutionary a foe and the free
   idea—its weapon. That's their fault.

5. People must leave this fear behind and go
   ahead. What's the sense to stick to the little
   you have now when you can have more tomorrow. Everything they must do is stretch
   their hands and feel for the new; give freedom to thoughts, ideas, to words.

6. For centuries each generation has been
   brought up in a same pattern. Ideals is
   what everybody follows. Individuality is
   forgotten. People think in a same way, following the cliché drilled in them in child-
   hood, the cliché-education for all children.
   And, when someone dares defy authority,
   he is punished and given as a bad example.
   "Here is what happens to you when you
   express your own opinion and deny your
   teacher's one".

7. Our society is sick and needs to be healed.
   The cure is a change in the system....

III. The System

1. The System. Centuries-old, existing on principles that hang no more today. A System that
   has not changed much since the day of its birth.

2. The System is wrong.

3. The System must impose its truth upon us
   so that it can rule. The government needs
   us to follow it blindly. For this reason we
   live in an informational eclipse. When
   people acquire information other than that
   from the government, they cannot distinguish the right from the wrong. So the lie
   becomes a truth—a truth, fundamental to
   everything else. Thus the leaders control
   with lies and the ordinary people have no

notion of what is true and follow the government blindly, trusting it.

4. We fight for freedom of information. We fight for freedom of speech and press. For the freedom to express our thoughts freely, without being persecuted by the System.

5. Even in the most-developed and 'democratic' countries, the system imposes misinformation. Even in the countries that pretend to be the cradle of free speech. Misinformation is one of the System's main weapons. A weapon, they use very well.

6. It is the Net that helps us spread the information freely. The Net, with no boundaries and information limit.

7. Ours is yours; yours is ours.

8. Everyone can share information; no restrictions.

9. Encrypting of information is our weapon. Thus the words of revolution can spread uninterrupted, and the government can only guess.

10. The Net is our realm. In the Net we are Kings

11. Laws. The world is changing, but the laws remain the same. The System is not changing, only a few details get redressed for the new time, but everything in the concept remains the same.

12. We need new laws. Laws, fitting the times we live in, with the world that surrounds us. Not laws build on the basis of the past. Laws, build for today, laws that will fit tomorrow.

13. The laws that only refrain us. Laws that badly need revision.

IV. The Vision

1. Some people do not care much about what happens globally. They care about what happens around them, in their micro-universe.

2. These people can only see a dark future, for they can only see the life they live now.

3. Others show some concern about the global affairs. They are interested in everything, in the future in perspective, in what is going to happen globally.

4. They have a more optimistic view. To them the future is cleaner and more beautiful, for they can see into it and they see a more mature man, a wiser world.

5. We are in the middle. We are interested in what happens now, and in what's gonna happen tomorrow as well.

6. We look in the Net, and the Net is growing wide and wider.

7. Soon everything in this world will be swallowed by the Net: from the military systems to the PC at home.

8. But the Net is a house of anarchy.

9. It cannot be controlled and in this is its power.

10. Every man will be dependent on the Net.

11. The whole information will be there, locked in the abysses of zeros and ones.

12. Who controls the Net, controls the information.

13. We will live in a mixture of past and present.

14. The bad come from the man, and the good comes from technology.

15. The Net will control the little man, and we will control the Net.

16. For if you do not control, you will be controlled.

17. The Information is POWER!

V. Where are we?

1. Where are we?

2. We all live in a sick world, where hatred is a weapon, and freedom—a dream.

3. The world grows so slowly. It is hard for a Cyberpunk to live in an underdeveloped world, looking at the people around him, seeing how wrongly they develop.

4. We go ahead, they pull us back again. Society suppresses us. Yes, it suppresses the freedom of thought. With its cruel education programs in schools and universities. They drill in the children their view of things and every attempt to express a different opinion is denied and punished.

5. Our kids grow educated in this old and still unchanged System. A System that tolerates no freedom of thought and demands a strict obeyance to the rules.

6. In what a world, how different from this, could we live now, if people were making jumps and not creeps.

7. It is so hard to live in this world, Cyberpunk.

8. It is as if time has stopped.

9. We live on the right spot, but not in the right time.

10. Everything is so ordinary, people are all the same, their deeds too. As if society feels an urgent need to live back in time.

11. Some, trying to find their own world, the world of a Cyberpunk, and finding it, build their own world. Build in their thoughts, it changes reality, lays over it and thus they live in a virtual world. The thought-up, build upon reality.

12. Others simply get accustomed to the world as it is. They continue to live in it, although they dislike it. They have no other choice but the bare hope that the world will go out of its hollow and will go ahead.

13. What we are trying to do is change the situation. We are trying to adjust the present world to our needs and views. To use maximally what is fit and to ignore the trash. Where we can't, we just live in this world, like Cyberpunks, no matter how hard, when society fights us we fight back.

14. We build our worlds in Cyberspace.

15. Among the zeros and ones, among the bits of information.

16. We build our community. The community of Cyberpunks.

Unite!

Fight for your rights!

Christian A. Kirtchev is Kristiyan's pen name.

Kristiyan Kirchev
A Cyberpunk Manifesto

Born in Eastern Europe, **Kristiyan Kirchev** grew up in the uncertainty of fallen communism and the exciting emerge of networked computer technologies.

Trained as a carpenter, Kristiyan mastered his cyber competencies hacking his way through the wild electronic frontier, while traveling the seas onboard a cargo ship.

Along with *A Cyberpunk Manifesto* Kristiyan has authored sci-fi stories in electronic 'zines and articles in media ecology, avatar fashion, and cybermind navigation. In Kristiyan's view the computer networks are only natural element of the evolution where the mind just like the computer serves as a tool in the transition to a greater existence, which in the future would be hardware independent, i.e. telepathy without phone and "knowing" without Googling. A couple of Kristiyan's on-line works, such as the "Desktop Exhibitions" posted in a Bulgarian web media, was juggling with issues such as computer screen desktop wallpapers replacing the actual paintings at home, and using the software icon as a paintbrush of expression in the boring office life.

kristiyan@gmail.com; http://k.cult.bg

Our genetic assignment is the receiving, processing, and producing of digital information.

Ronin Books for Independent

THE FIGUTIVE PHILOSOPHER..Leary/FIGPHI $12.95 ___
From Harvard Professor to fugitive—the amazing story.

PSYCHEDELIC PRAYERS...Leary/PSYPRA $12.95 ___
Guide to transcendental experience based on Tao Te Ching

PSYCHEDELIC PRAYERS—Keepsake Edition...........................Leary $20.00 ___
Hard cover—makes a great gift for 60s enthusiast

HIGH PRIEST...Leary/HIGPRI $19.95 ___
Acid trips lead by Huxley, Ginsburg, Burroughs, Ram Dass and other 60s gurus

HIGH PRIEST—Collector's Edition..................................Leary $100.00 ___
Limited edition in hard cover, numbered and signed by Timothy Leary

POLITICS OF ECSTASY..Leary/POLECS $14.95 ___
Classic, the book that got Leary called the "most dangerous man in America"

CHANGE YOUR BRAIN..LearyCHAYOU $12.95 ___
Brain change is more taboo than sex and why

DISCORDIA...DISCORD $14.00 ___
Parody of religion based upon Eris, goddess of chaos & confusion.

EVOULTIONARY AGENTS:...Leary/EVOAGE $12.95 ___
Leary's future history. Why the only smart thing to do is to get smarter.

POLITICS OF SELF-DETERMINATION...................................Leary/POLSEL $12.95 ___
Leary's pre-Harvard years & his *real* claim to fame that got him to Harvard.

MUSINGS ON HUMAN METAMORPHOSES ....Leary/MUSING $12.95 ___
Spin psychology. Mutants and malcontents migrate first. The only place to go is up!

THE WAY OF THE RONIN..Potter/WAYRON $14.95 ___
Maverick career strategy for riding the waves of chaos at work.

POLITICS OF PSYCHOPHARMOCOLOGY.................Leary/POLPSY $12.95 ___
Story of Tim's persecution for his ideas including interrogation by Teddy Kennedy.

CHAOS AND CYBER CULTURE..Leary/CHACYB $29.95 ___
Cyberpunk manifesto on designing chaos and fashioning personal disorders

START YOUR OWN RELIGION....................................... Leary/STAREL $14.00 ___
Gather your cult, write your own New Testiment, select your sacrament.

> **Books prices: SUBTOTAL** $_____
>
> CA customers add sales tax 8.75%   _____
>
> **BASIC SHIPPING: (All orders)**   **$6.00**

PLUS SHIPPING: USA+$1/bk, Canada+$2/bk, Europe+$6/bk, Pacific+$8/bk _____

Books + Tax + Basic shipping + Shipping per book: TOTAL $_____

Check/MO payable to **Ronin Publishing**

MC __ Visa __ Discover __ Exp date _ _ / _ _ card #:___/____/____/____

Signature _____

Ronin Publishing, Inc • Box 22900 • Oakland, CA 94609
Ph:800/858.2665 • Fax:510/420-3672
www.roninpub.com for online catalog
Price & availability subject to change without notice

Reboot Your Brain
Change Reality
Screens